NEW WAYS
TO HEALTH

P9-CEH-739

# HOMEOPATHY

## STIMULATING THE BODY'S NATURAL IMMUNE SYSTEM

BY

### SARAH RICHARDSON, RS HOM

FOREWORD BY

### ROBERT SCHILLER, M.D.

PREFACE BY

### WILLIAM SHEVIN, M.D.

PRESIDENT, THE

### NATIONAL CENTER FOR HOMEOPATHY, WASHINGTON, D.C.

### HARMONY BOOKS

### NEW YORK

Published by Harmony Books, a division of Crown Publishers, Inc., 225 Park Avenue South, New York, New York 10003.

Originally published in Great Britain in 1988 by The Hamlyn Publishing Group Limited, a division of the Octopus Publishing Group,

HARMONY and colophon are trademarks of Crown Publishers, Inc.

Printed and bound in Hong Kong

**Library of Congress Cataloging-in-Publication Data**

Richardson, Sarah
    Homeopathy: Stimulating the Body's Natural
    Immune System
    (New ways to health)
    Bibliography: p.
    Includes Index.

    1. Homeopathy – Popular works. I. Title.
    II. Series: New ways to health book.
    RX76.R53   1989
    615.5'32

88-16587

ISBN 0-517-57148-X

10 9 8 7 6 5 4 3 2 1

First Edition

**Publisher's Note:** This book is designed as a source guide for readers to use when deciding whether to participate in an overall homeopathic program. The decision to seek health advice from a homeopath is individual choice.

# CONTENTS

# FOREWORD

I came to homeopathy the way many doctors do. I used it to treat myself. After taking a medical seminar in homeopathy, I soon had occasion to try it. Carrying a huge bundle of medical journals out to the garbage, I tripped down the stairs and injured my ankle. Cursing those volumes for causing me pain rather than giving me guidance to heal others, I decided to try my new knowledge of homeopathy, and used the remedy *Arnica*. This was not a study; there is no way to know what the outcome would have been without the homeopathy. However, my ankle healed in one day.

Since then I have developed clinical confidence in this remarkable approach to healing. It is effective not only for treating a multitude of common medical problems, but it can enhance the immune system and prevent illness as well.

Homeopathy offers an accessible, effective alternative to conventional medical treatment that promotes self-care and uses remedies with minimal side effects. After gaining some experience under the supervision of a trained practitioner, most people can use it to easily treat a wide range of health problems at home. And, as presently manufactured, homeopathic remedies are significantly less expensive than their conventional counterparts.

Increasing numbers of people are seeking out alternative medicines as a result of frustration with our standard health care system or with the system's failure to help them. Alternative approaches to medicine fulfill a deep need by offering practical therapeutic answers in a more sensitive, individualized fashion. Homeopathy is one of the more promising of these therapies and deserves a wider audience and an important position in a new, comprehensive, more humanistic medical system. With her book, *Homeopathy: Stimulating the Body's Natural Immune System*, Sarah Richardson has performed a great service by providing us with a clear, useful summary of this vital medical tradition.

Robert Schiller, M.D.

# PREFACE

Homeopathy is medicine on the human scale. It is probably the simplest of the complementary therapies for people without specialist knowledge to understand. The central tenet – that like cures like – is a simple, satisfying idea that is easy to grasp. The homeopathic vocabulary is pleasingly uncluttered with medical terms; indeed, the language of homeopathy is simply the description of the experience of disease in the human body, something which is part of everyone's life and therefore accessible to all.

Homeopathy is also about individuals: each diagnosis is specific and each remedy is precisely tailored to the patient's symptoms. In other words, the patient is part of the cure.

So it is not surprising that growing numbers of people are turning to homeopathy as part of the general shift towards taking more responsibility for one's own health. An essential part of this responsibility is self-education.

*Homeopathy: Stimulating the Body's Natural Immune System* will be an indispensable aid to self-education. In a clear, informative text, Sarah Richardson provides a sound basic introduction to this therapy: she covers the history of the idea of homeopathy, discusses the work and dedication of its founder Dr Samuel Hahnemann and in more practical terms, explains how homeopathic diagnoses are built up, how the remedies are made, and describes the experience of homeopathic treatment through different case histories.

As a practising homeopathic physician with orthodox training and experience, I know that homeopathy works; rather than merely suppressing symptoms, it actually makes people healthier. Its potential, within medicine, is enormous. *Homeopathy: Stimulating the Body's Natural Immune System* shows you why this is and how homeopathy can work for you.

William Shevin, MD, D.Ht
President, the National Center for
Homeopathy, Washington DC

# 1

# INTRODUCTION

Homeopathy is a system of medical therapy that concentrates on care of the whole person by methods that are gentle and sympathetic to the body's needs. It developed from investigations carried out in the eighteenth and early nineteenth centuries by a German physician, Dr Samuel Hahnemann. This development has been generally independent of other kinds of therapy, but homeopathy is, in many ways, complementary to other systems of health care, including Western orthodox medicine. And although conventional doctors cannot explain exactly how homeopathy works, work it does – often with quite dramatic and remarkable results.

*The Physician's highest calling, his only calling, is to make sick people healthy – to heal, as it is termed.*

Samuel Hahnemann

### What does 'homeopathy' mean?

The word homeopathy was coined by Hahnemann from two Greek words, *homoios* (like) and *pathos* (suffering). The first syllable is pronounced to rhyme with Tom, and has nothing to do with the Latin *homo* (man). Hahnemann's word neatly sums up one of the basic principles of homeopathy, which had been expressed for centuries in medical treatises by the Latin tag *similia similibus curantur,* meaning 'like is cured by like'. In contrast, orthodox medicine is generally based on the principle of opposites, so Hahnemann coined the word 'allopathy', from the Greek *allos* (other), to describe its principles.

### Like cures like, and the minimum dose

Together with the principle of 'like cures like' homeopathy couples a second, equally important, concept: the use of the minimum dose. The appropriateness of homeopathic medicines has been determined by monitoring the effects of various substances on healthy people. This is known as 'proving'. A patient who displays signs and symptoms *similar* to those produced by the large dose is given a minimum dose of the same substance, to stimulate his or her body's own defence systems. Briefly, the illness and the remedy that is prescribed to treat it produce a similar set of symptoms. The key word is 'similar', not 'the same'. Note that 'symptoms' are felt and detected by patients themselves, whereas 'signs' are the outward manifestations that a practitioner sees when examining patients.

One major advantage of homeopathy is its safety. While its medicines are powerful in action, working *with* the body's own defences, their actual measurable strength is too low to give rise to the undesirable side-effects that many modern drugs produce in orthodox medicine, which requires larger doses to be prescribed.

## The homeopathic view of disease

A central principle of homeopathic diagnosis and treatment concerns the signs and symptoms of a disease. Homeopathic practitioners regard them as expressions of the way in which the body itself is endeavouring to combat disease. They see them as positive indications of the body's attempt to maintain the status quo, rather than manifestations of the disease itself, which is the way that other medical systems tend to regard them.

This view of illness leads naturally to the way in which a homeopath looks upon somebody who is ill. Rather than seeing their patients as mere objects, exhibiting particular pathological symptoms, homeopaths look first at the person as a whole. This is because they recognize that, if symptoms reflect the patient's physical response to illness (rather then the illness itself), it is necessary to take account of everything about the patient before the symptoms can be correctly understood. A particular patient may exhibit different signs and symptoms in response to a disease such as a cold at different times. The signs and symptoms depend on the person's age, general health and vitality, previous medical history and even state of mind.

If you have a strong vitality and basic good health, then when you fall ill your body's ability to heal itself is likely to be good. You will quickly throw off the cold or whatever the complaint is. Typically, you experience temporary symptoms indicating that your system is attempting to return to health, but they follow a predictably improving course. This is especially so if you are able to rest, and take other appropriate steps to allow your immune system to do its job.

On the other hand, if you catch a cold when you are already feeling run down and depressed, the composite healing process is far more complicated – resulting in a cold that is much harder to shake off.

According to homeopathic principles, seeking help with this healing process is necessary only when your own self-healing mechanism fails, and is unable to complete the normal process of returning you to your usual state of health. That is when you need homeopathy.

# 2

# HOW CAN HOMEOPATHY HELP?

Britain's Royal Family and members of the European aristocracy have supported homeopathy since the 1830s. And many other well-known people – including Yehudi Menuhin, Tina Turner, John D. Rockefeller, Sr., and Mother Theresa – have all discovered that homeopathy produces positive, lasting results.

Yet despite their efficacy and safety, so-called 'alternative' therapies often represent the last resort of a desperate person. Years of unsuccessful orthodox treatment for conditions such as hayfever, asthma, and eczema frequently preceed the first visit to a homeopathic doctor or practitioner. More elusive diseases, such as Myalgic Encephalomyelitis or Post-Viral Fatigue Syndrome (known in the US as Chronic Fatigue Syndrome), may evade conventional diagnostic methods because there is no obvious clinical proof.

But it would be foolish to ignore the wide range of non-specific disorders which afflict humanity simply because we are, as yet, unable to identify them in a laboratory. The homeopathic approach avoids such pitfalls by seeing each patient as an individual who is displaying certain symptoms. Rather than labelling the disease, a homeopath seeks to discover the underlying cause of the problem. This may be mental, emotional, physical, spiritual or a combination of these factors. Homeopathy has been using what is now called a holistic approach for two hundred years – because it works.

*Ask not what kind of illness the patient has, ask what kind of patient has the illness.*

Sir William Osler

### Understanding holistic healing

Many ancient systems of medicine were founded on holistic principles. Hippocrates, for instance, paid close attention to his patients' dreams during the healing process as long ago as the 4th century B.C. Today, Chinese acupuncture is perhaps the best-known example of a holistic system which has not only survived for thousands of years, but is now gaining widespread orthodox acceptance in the Western world.

Homeopathy is holistic because it considers the whole person. Few people would dispute the reality of their body, their emotions or their mental processes. And although the existence of a soul may appear to be a mystical concept, it is difficult to deny the presence of some kind of animating force which departs at the point of death. Orthodox medicine typically classifies disease as being mental *or* physical *or* emotional. In holistic and homeopathic terms, aspects of all diseases manifest themselves at every level – and total health

## THE WHOLE BEING

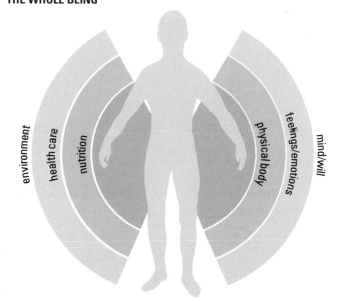

environment

health care

nutrition

physical body

feelings/emotions

mind/will

*HRH The Queen Mother has always been a supporter of homeopathic medicine, as has Sir Yehudi Menuhin (above left).*

*We all have our own genetically determined constitution, which dictates our optimum health level. Homeo-pathy looks beyond the outward physical aspect, believing that the mind and will are the most powerful aspects of the person, followed by the emotions and lastly the physical body.*

and well-being depend upon harmony and balance being present on each plane of being.

Premenstrual Syndrome, for example, affects a great number of women mentally, physically and emotionally. So, although this condition may result from temporary hormonal imbalance or inadequate nutrition, it also creates emotional and mental imbalance. Similarly, stress reactions such as sweating, racing heartbeat, and loss of appetite are frequently physical manifestations of inner emotional and mental turmoil. And it is now generally agreed that prolonged stress is a prime factor in many diseases such as cancer, and heart conditions.

So, despite a certain amount of sceptical resistance from the medical establishment, holistic healing methods are being taken more seriously. In a lecture given in Montreal, Canada, in 1984 British M.P., Dr. David Owen, called for a return to holistic medicine:

> 'The holistic approach is not a new fangled trendy manifestation of quirky cults and way-out opinions. It is the reassertion of the traditional medical values where a sensitivity to the individuality of the person is a precious part of the practice of the healing profession.
> We have forgotten that the practice of medicine involves the whole person. We have fragmented responsibility for treatment . . . we are in danger of fragmenting our values and our purpose. It is time to reassert the wholeness of medicine, to do so in the way we teach medicine and practice medicine at every level.'

The roots of homeopathic practice are firmly founded in ancient half-forgotten wisdom. And as modern research methods become more and more sophisticated, holistic healing is gaining both scientific acceptance and public popularity. Indeed, homeopathy and other, complementary, therapies could well be the medicines of the future.

### Who can homeopathy help?

Homeopathy is a sophisticated system of medicine which can effectively treat adults, children, animals and plants. It can also, in many instances, be used as a complementary therapy when orthodox treatment, such as surgery, is a necessary procedure. There are more than 2,000 homeopathic remedies in use – and new medicines are still being

*The noise, bustle and general cut and thrust of modern life can have an adverse effect on many people, putting them under a stress that weakens their systems and predisposes them to illness. Help yourself to stay healthy by monitoring your stress levels – everybody has a different breaking point – and try to adapt your life, if possible, by changing your habits.*

researched and added to this long list. The way in which
these medicines are made is described in detail in Chapters 4
and 5. A wide range of substances (among them metals,
minerals, plants, insects, reptiles, chemical compounds and
animal products) have been tested (or 'proved') homeopathically and are included in the homeopathic *Materia Medica* -
which lists characteristic symptoms associated with each
remedy. Whatever your complaint homeopathic treatment
can help your body in its efforts to cure itself.

### Chronic and acute disease

Hahnemann's observation of disease led him to define two
general classes which he called acute and chronic, describing
an acute disease as follows: 'Such affections usually run their
course within a brief period of variable duration, and are
called acute diseases.' Influenza, for instance, would be classified as an acute illness. Chronic diseases, however, are
deep-rooted conditions which usually worsen with time.
This class of illness includes inherited tendencies, and sus-
ceptibilities such as asthma and arthritis. Both categories of
illness respond well to homeopathy, but while an acute condition may clear up rapidly, chronic disease involves complex causes which take time to unravel and heal.

### Homeopathy and the Common Cold

The majority of people will suffer from colds at some time
in their lives, and many of us regularly 'catch' colds every
winter. This acute illness has puzzled research scientists for
decades, for they have so far failed to find a cure. Homeopathy can often help in such cases, either by preventing a
cold occurring in the first place, or by methodically itemiz-
ing individual symptoms and prescribing a remedy on the
basis of 'like cures like'.

Homeopathy recognizes that the tendency to catch colds
springs from many different causes, inherited or acquired
later in life. For example, since the widespread use of the
tuberculosis vaccine (BCG), many people have had a layer
of tubercular weakness grafted on to their basic constitution
which makes them more likely to catch colds. Homeopathic
doses of *tuberculinum* will help combat this weakness.

The type of cold you catch depends on the effect of
viruses or bacteria on the underlying constitution as well as
any specific exciting causes. If they are to be successful,
homeopathic cold remedies must be chosen especially care-

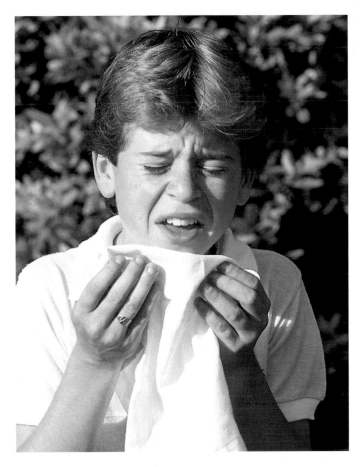

*The discomfort and misery of the common cold afflicts people of all ages. Orthodox treatment merely suppresses the symptoms. The homeopathic approach takes into account the type of cold it is and the underlying constitution of the cold victim.*

fully, according to your individual signs and symptoms, to find the correct remedy for you.

Whatever kind of cold it is, homeopathically speaking, the right remedy taken at the right time will do much to reduce discomfort and clear up the cold as soon as possible.

*Aconitum 30*, for example, would be appropriate for a sudden chill accompanied by a dry, painful cough made worse by cold, dry weather. Fever, sleeplessness, and a heavy, bursting headache are also *Aconitum* symptoms. *Gelsemium 30,* another common cold remedy, is used to treat a very different set of symptoms. A person with a typical *Gelsemium* cold would be feeling extremely drowsy, with heavy, drooping eyelids. Their cold is likely to have developed slowly, especially in damp mild weather, and will be accompanied by chilliness up and down the back, a lack of hunger and thirst, pain at the back of the head and a stuffy nose. There are many other remedies as well, depending on the kind of cold.

**Natural defences**

Allopathic medicine tends to treat colds and 'flu by suppressing their characteristic symptoms. Homeopaths have observed that this drives the illness deeper into the body, where it is likely to become more serious. A rise in temperature, or slight fever, frequently accompanies a bad cold and is conventionally suppressed with anti-inflammatory drugs such as aspirin. But fever is part of the body's defence mechanism. Studies undertaken since the mid 1970s have shown that, not surprisingly, fever is actually a healthy response to bacterial or viral invasion. American physiologist, Matthew Kluger, has been investigating fever at the University of Michigan Medical School and has shown that it is one of the ways our bodies adapt to resist infection.

A high temperature is a by-product of your body fighting infection by increasing the number of white blood cells. As these cells become more active, they produce more interferon, which is a body protein that prevents an increase in viral growth. (Of course, a prolonged bout of very high fever can be dangerous and needs to be treated appropriately. There are many homeopathic remedies for high fever, depending on the particular signs and symptoms of the condition.)

Catarrhal discharge is also frequently suppressed by decongestants and nasal sprays. Again, such conventional methods are not helping the body – and may even excacerbate a straightforward cold, especially in children. Catarrh represents toxic waste, which the body is throwing out. It contains dead white blood cells, bacteria, viruses and mucus and, quite simply, is better out than in. Homeopathic treatment can reduce the incidence of frequent colds by ensuring that the body clears itself completely, without inhibiting its natural defence mechanisms.

**Homeopathy and allergies**

Allergies seem to be on the increase. Recent statistics show that one in seven Americans had an allergy in 1950 – by 1985 this figure had increased to one in three, or 75 million people. More sophisticated diagnostic techniques may perhaps partially explain this statistic, for seasonal allergies, such as hayfever, were often thought to be summer colds. Indeed, the acute stage of an allergic reaction does superficially resemble a violent cold. Repeated sneezing, watering eyes and a runny nose are common allergic reactions brought about by an over-reaction of the immune system to the allergen, or foreign body.

Household chemicals, pollen, cosmetics, animal hairs and food are all capable of triggering allergy attacks in sensitive people. Asthma and eczema, which make many people's lives a misery, are also defined as allergic reactions – although they can also be brought on by stress and emotional states. Homeopaths regard allergies as being symptomatic of a fundamental chronic condition, and seek to strengthen the body's overall resistance. Professional homeopathic care can, in many cases, reduce allergy attacks – or eradicate them altogether.

*This idyllic carpet of summer flowers brings nothing but trepidation to the heart of a hay fever sufferer. Orthodox medicine combats hay fever with anti-histamine drugs, which suppress the body's immune system. Unfortunately, this treatment has side-effects such as drowsiness and, of course, temporarily lowers the body's natural resistance to infection.*

## Hay fever

Hay fever is a recurrent seasonal allergy to pollen. Conventionally, it is usually treated with antihistamines which, although they effectively suppress allergic symptoms, neither cure the illness nor provide longterm relief. In addition, side effects such as drowsiness can make it dangerous to drive, or operate machinery.

If you suffer from hay fever, homeopathy could be the answer. An interesting study of hay fever was undertaken in 1986 at the Glasgow Homeopathic Hospital, in collaboration with the University of Glasgow. One hundred and forty-four hay fever sufferers were chosen for the experiment – some were given a placebo, while others were given a homeopathic medicine consisting of twelve types of grass pollen. These patients showed six times as much improvement as those who took the placebo; proving that not only can homeopathy lessen hay fever symptoms but also that it cannot be dismissed as a placebo response.

## Asthma and eczema

Asthma and eczema often begin in childhood, and may or may not be outgrown by the time a sufferer reaches maturity. These illnesses frequently appear together, and are known to be linked. Homeopaths believe that suppression of childish eczema with steroid creams can cause the disease to be driven into the body, from whence it will re-emerge as asthma at a later date.

Asthma may prove difficult to treat homeopathically because of longterm use of suppressant drugs. It is particularly difficult to get a clear homeopathic 'picture' of an adult asthmatic who has a long history of conventional medication. Many homeopaths are in fact not keen on their patients giving up their inhalers (used during acute attacks), as sudden withdrawal would complicate the picture too much. Instead, they are gradually weaned off and a suitable homeopathic remedy substituted. Therefore homeopathic treatment for adults is a long term undertaking. However, the story is different with children. If they are seen early enough, it is possible to control the asthma without recourse to a lifetime's dependency on inhalers.

Asthma and eczema are closely linked. It is important to note that as asthma improves (in asthma/eczema sufferers) eczema eruptions may temporarily worsen. These eruptions should not be suppressed, otherwise the asthma will

*A Ventolin inhaler is orthodox medicine's treatment for acute asthma attacks. Asthmatic children easily learn how to use it for themselves when they feel an attack coming on. The inhaler propels, into the windpipe, the drug salbumatol which dilates the air passages.*

re-emerge and the vicious circle will never be broken.

Nobody knows what causes eczema, but it is often inherited. Psychological factors such as anxiety and stress seem to contribute to the severity of attacks, and eczema sufferers may also experience other allergies such as hay fever. A homeopath will want to know whether the eczema is worse at night, or in damp weather. Where the inflammation occurs is also important, for this helps to determine which remedy is prescribed. By improving overall levels of health, homeopathy can provide constructive help.

## Homeopathy, pregnancy and birth

Many modern mothers are now seeking safer medical care during pregnancy, labour, and while breast-feeding their babies – and this is an area where homeopathy can certainly provide a valid option. There are safe, effective homeopathic remedies for morning sickness, breathlessness, swollen ankles (oedema) and heartburn, none of which can harm

*Breast is undoubtedly best for both mother and baby. If all goes well, breast milk delivers nourishing, well-balanced food at the right temperature in just the right amounts.*

*If there are problems, orthodox medicine often combats them with antibiotics, which the mother passes on to the baby. Homeopathic remedies, which are prescribed after a detailed investigation into the mother's emotional and physical state, have no such side-effects.*

the baby or cause side effects worse than the complaint.

Homeopathic remedies are also invaluable during labour, for they can be used to strengthen the mother physically and mentally, decrease delivery time, and speed up recovery after the birth. Three French researchers published the results of a double-blind trial in 1987 which tested five homeopathic medicines commonly used to aid labour. A double-blind trial is one where neither the patients nor the doctor administering the medicine know which substance is being used. In this way, it is argued, independent assessment of its action is assured. It is very difficult to judge homeopathic remedies by this method because they are generally prescribed on an individual basis.

However, this particular trial successfully showed that *Caulophyllum* (blue cohosh) decreased both birth time and difficulties during labour. The women who were given homeopathic medicines were in labour for an average of 5.1 hours, while those who received a placebo averaged 8.5 hours. *Caulophyllum* has such a reputation for speeding up the process of childbirth that it must never be self-administered, for it is known to bring on premature labour.

After the baby is born, homeopathy can help with breast-feeding problems, post-natal depression and post-natal incontinence.

### Homeopathic care of babies and children

Babies and children respond well to homeopathy, which has the important added benefit of producing no damaging side-effects. It can help with colic in newborn babies, which can be distressing for infant and parents alike. Some homeopathic doctors and practitioners specialize in this field, which can be especially helpful for problems such as hyperactivity.

Conventional medicine, modern hygiene and nutrition have certainly helped to reduce the incidence of infant mortality. And many children now survive thanks to the antibiotics and advanced surgical techniques which are available today. Yet such dramatic medical intervention is unnecessary for common childhood problems like teething, minor infections, or colds. Indiscriminate use of antibiotics may even be dangerous – tetracycline, for instance, can affect bone growth, cause liver damage, and cause unsightly permanent stains on children's teeth. For these reasons the American Academy of Pediatrics has advised against the use

*Homeopaths are very successful at treating children, and some of them specialize in homeopathic paediatrcis. The treament is non-invasive and the remedies free from side effects.*

*The sleepless nights and disrupted days that characterize hyper-activity are distressing. Although hyperactive behaviour is often associated with food intolerance, it is sometimes difficult to pin down the guilty food.*

of this popular antibiotic when treating children under eight years of age.

Homeopathy can be particularly effective in dealing with the after-effects of vaccination. One of the main effects of the vaccines, which have prevented many children from falling victim to whooping cough, polio, diphtheria and tetanus, is increased catarrh and mucus production. This has resulted in many children suffering from 'glue ear', as the mucus collects in the space in the middle ear. While this is not life-threatening, it leads to a significant degree of deafness, usually different in each ear. The orthodox response to this is the insertion of grommets, small drainage tubes, in the ear. Homeopathic treatment however, carried out early enough after the vaccinations will help to avoid the grommet insertion.

### The treatment of animals

While many animal-lovers may insist that their dog or cat has its own personality, the animals themselves are unable to provide vets or owners with detailed psychological information. When homeopathy effectively treats pets and livestock, therefore, it cannot be explained away as a form of faith-healing. Moreover veterinary homeopathy is on the increase worldwide as vets explore the possibilities of a number of holistic therapies, including acupuncture and massage for animals.

In 1984 Christopher Day, a British vet, published the results of an experiment with pigs. All the sows suffered from a high incidence of stillbirths – so *Caulophyllum* was given to some pigs, while others were given a placebo. *Caulophyllum* was shown to reduce stillbirths in these pigs by 10 percent.

Most domestic pets including dogs, cats, hamsters, birds and tortoises all happily respond to homeopathy. And since treating animals is quite straightforward, many simple ailments can be successfully dealt with at home. Clearly, serious or persistent symptoms such as vomiting will need professional care – but otherwise it is safe and economical to use homeopathic preparations for your pets.

Careful observation of the animal's behaviour, combined with an objective pathological diagnosis are required when prescribing for pets and livestock. Is the animal pining? Does it seem worse at night, or during the day? Do symptoms improve with sleep, or with exercise? Answers to

*Homeopathic vet Christopher Day attends to the needs of Dahlia the pig. The success of homeopathic medicine for animals supports the case for homeopathy as an objective therapy.*

these questions, and many others like them, are an essential part of accurate homeopathic prescribing – for both humans and animals. *Ignatia*, for example, is often recommended for pining animals – whether they have lost their litter, or are reacting badly to boarding kennels. In humans, *ignatia* symptoms include grief, anxiety and fear – exactly what an unhappy animal may be suffering.

### How you can help yourself
Self-responsibility and a willingness to change are key factors in homeopathic healing. And no system of medicine can cure you completely if you refuse to co-operate. A nutritious diet, adequate rest, and sufficient exercise are all generally acknowledged to be necessary for continued good health and vitality. Positive mental attitudes also play an important role in health maintenance. Indeed, recent research by Professor Paul Ekman at the University of California indicates that smiling beneficially affects our autonomic nervous system – decreasing both heart rate and blood pressure.

*Human beings are sociable animals, and many 'diseases' are the result of, or exacerbated by, loneliness and isolation. One of the ways to help yourself to good health is to maintain an interest in other people and to cultivate your friendships.*

Samuel Hahnemann, the founder of homeopathy, said 'treat the cause' – and if you are damaging your body by eating too many junk foods, then a homeopath will insist on a change of diet. Some homeopaths recommend controlled fasting on fruit and vegetables to help eliminate toxins from the body – while others may suggest a milk and vegetable diet be followed for a time. Homeopaths are not dieticians, but recognize that food may frequently be a contributory cause of disease. By eating a sensible, balanced diet of whole foods – including fresh fruit and vegetables – you can greatly improve your energy levels, and your general resistance to infection overall.

Accepting responsibility for your thoughts and emotions is another important area for consideration. Mental techniques including creative visualization, meditation and

## A BALANCED DIET

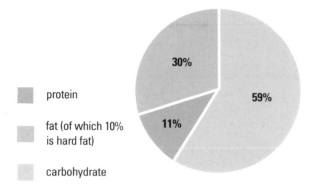

30%

59%

11%

protein

fat (of which 10% is hard fat)

carbohydrate

*A healthy, well-balanced diet goes a long way towards preventing digestive disorders. People in the affluent West often suffer needlessly because they fuel themselves with too much prepackaged and 'junk' food. Aim for a diet that includes plenty of fresh fruit and vegetables, whole foods and lean fish and meat. Your daily intake should comprise 11 per cent protein, 30 per cent fat (of which only 10 per cent should be hard, saturated fat) and 59 per cent carbohydrate taken in the form of fruit, vegetables, wholemeal pasta and bread products.*

positive thinking can be powerful tools in the fight against disease. They can also help to keep you well by teaching you how to control negative emotions and stress reactions. A great deal of scientific evidence demonstrates that meditation, for example, lowers both breathing and metabolic rates – and measurably reduces feelings of anxiety and aggression. There are many types of meditation and other mind control techniques, ranging from classical disciplines such as yoga to modern methods like autogenic training. It is worth sampling some of these techniques to see which of them fits in best with your life. Any of them can be safely used in conjunction with homeopathic treatment.

Many temporary nervous conditions – fear of flying, exam nerves  can be helped homeopathically. Remedies depend, as ever, on your particular symptoms.

### Homeopathy at home

Common minor problems are easily treated at home with homeopathy – and many homeopathic pharmacies supply ready-made first aid kits for home use. It must be emphasized that any persistent or distressing symptoms require professional care – but day-to-day domestic upsets will readily respond to homeopathic remedies.

As a general rule, four or five doses should produce results – remember to stop taking the remedy as soon as you can see an improvement. For acute conditions, these doses may be taken at half-hourly intervals, increasing to once every two or three hours as improvement occurs. Homeopathic remedies are subtle and sensitive – so wait for twenty to thirty minutes after eating before you take them. This rule applies before meals too. Peppermint toothpaste, camphor, tobacco and coffee can also interfere with their action, so avoid using these substances half an hour before and after taking medicine as well. Special, bland homeopathic toothpaste is available in some pharmacies for this reason.

Keep your remedies out of direct sunlight, in a cool, dry place where they will not come in contact with any strong-smelling substances which could damage them. Carefully stored they should last a long time; some experts maintain that they may even be effective after 50 years.

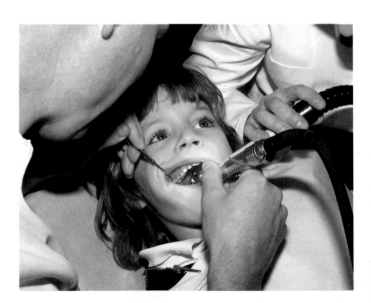

*Homeopathy can provide remedies to help those chronically afraid of the drill to face up to dental treatment, and to deal with any slight discomfort afterwards.*

## HOMEOPATHIC FIRST AID

*Here are a few suggestions for homeopathic self-help. There are also several clearly-written books describing indications for the use of remedies, which are essential reading for any homeopathic household.*

## BRUISED MUSCLES

*Arnica 30* taken internally, *Arnica* ointment applied externally to unbroken skin. *Arnica* also helps to reduce any shock symptoms.

## BRUISED BONES AND STRAINED LIGAMENTS

*Ruta 6* taken internally four times a day. *Ruta graveolens* ointment may be used externally.

## CUTS AND GRAZES

One part *Calendula-Hypericum* tincture to ten parts tepid water is used to clean the wound, before applying a plaster. Small cuts may not require dressing – in which case *Calendula* ointment may be used to soothe and heal.

## BITES AND STINGS

Use *Calendula-Hypericum* tincture for mosquito bites. *Ledum* or *Hypericum* tincture will soothe puncture wounds made by insects. Use *Cantharis 6* or *Apis 6* (made from crushed bees) taken internally if the skin is swollen and burning.

## THE DENTIST – BEFORE AND AFTER

Countless adults and children are terrified of the dentist. *Ignatia 30*, taken an hour before your visit will help to calm those fearful feelings. If you have had a tooth taken out, *Hypericum 30* taken as needed speeds recovery. *Arnica 30* is helpful if your jaw or teeth feel bruised after filling. And once healing is underway, a mouthwash made from one part *Calendula-Hypericum* tincture to ten parts warm water is very soothing.

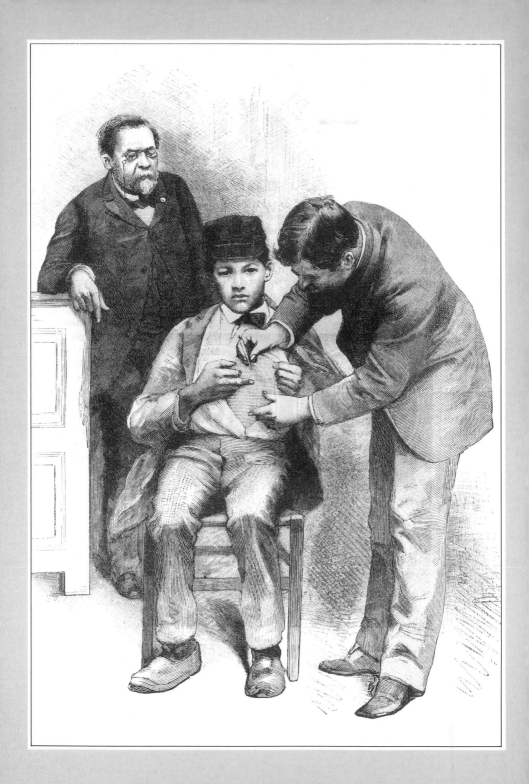

# 3

# HOMEOPATHY
# IN CONTEXT

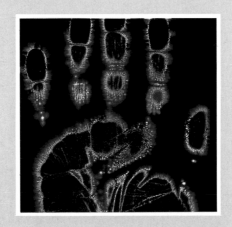

The human body is a miracle of complex biological engineering. It is capable of producing painkillers, replacing dead cells, and resisting viral and bacterial invasion. So, what goes wrong – and why do we need medicines at all? Stress, inherited weakness, and environmental factors may all be responsible for bouts of illness – for physiologically we have not completely adapted to civilization.

*A single symptom is no more the whole disease than a single foot is a whole man.*

Samuel Hahnemann

We consume large numbers of chemicals, breathe polluted air, suppress our emotions and generally subject our bodies, and ourselves, to more abuse than they are meant to take. Sooner or later, our delicately-balanced systems begin to show signs of strain, and we fall ill. British homeopath, Dr. Trevor Smith, suggested in a recent article that 'stress is a major factor in about 70% of the cases that are seen and, in some practices, particularly in the inner city areas, it can rise to as high as 80%, possibly 85%'. Stress – whether rooted in psychological or physical causes – can be a killer.

Scientist Hans Seyle, who pioneered research into stress during the 1930s, defined it as 'the non-specific response of the body to any demand made upon it.' His research revealed that our stress reactions can be divided into three stages: alarm, or 'fight or flight syndrome'; resistance or adaptation; and finally – exhaustion. He also observed that some of us cope better than others when subjected to stress. Why should this be so? Seyle believed that this was due to two factors – how we consciously adapt to difficulties and challenges, and our individual inherited systemic weaknesses.

## Miasms and inherited weakness

Hahnemann spent twelve years investigating inherited systemic weakness, and susceptibility to various kinds of illness. Puzzled by persistent recurrent patterns of disease in some of his patients, he set out to 'gradually solve this sublime problem through unremitting thought, indefatigable inquiry, faithful observation and the most accurate experiments.' The result was his theory of miasms.

As we now know, basic genetic structural patterns pass from one generation to the next. Diseases such as haemophilia are transmitted in this way – and researchers have observed how heart disease, diabetes and schizophrenia seem to run in families too. A predisposition to certain types of illness is called a susceptibility; it maintains a lowered state of health through a weakness in an individual's defence

*City life may be exciting but it brings its own disadvantages – alienation, overcrowding and frequently a stressful and tense lifestyle. There is a very narrow dividing line between stimulation and stress, and inner city stress has been proved to be a major factor in disease suffered by urban populations.*

system. When an exciting cause – such as bacteria or a virus – enters that individual's life, he may succumb to disease. If twenty people were exposed to the same exciting causes, they would not all respond in the same way – simply because their central states of susceptibility differ.

Hahnemann's miasms are difficult to explain because, as with many other homeopathic beliefs, they cannot be analysed by current scientific technology. However, they are fundamental to a complete understanding of homeopathy as a system of medicine. The way in which Hahnemann formulated his theory of miasms is described more fully in Chapter 7, but the main principles are summarized here.

Originally, three basic miasms were identified, each with their own set of symptoms. Hahnemann considered these to be the underlying causes of all chronic conditions. Since

*Franz Schubert (1797-1828) the composer died tragically young from typhoid fever. He never really recovered from the syphilis he contracted six years before his death, and it is probable that his constitution was undermined by an inherited syphilitic miasm.*

Hahnemann's day, different diseases (such as TB, cancer) orthodox treatment (vaccines, drugs) and pollution have produced new miasmic layers. Combinations of these miasms, and a large number of subsequent ones, have since been discovered – but the three original ones were:

**Psoric miasm** - or 'the itch'. Hahnemann believed this to be a virtually universal layer of weakness in mankind.

**Syphilitic miasm** – inherited weakness due to syphilis. This weakness can be transmitted from one generation to another. Historically, countless people contracted syphilis, which was a common affliction in Hahnemann's day.

**Sycotic miasm** - inherited weakness due to gonorrhoea.

It is important to realize that a venereal miasm is not caused by microbes. If you are diagnosed as suffering from the syphilitic miasm, for example, it does not mean that one of your parents was diseased. But one of their ancestors suffered from syphilis, and this particular type of weakness has been passed on to you.

Repeated acute illnesses point to an underlying chronic state or miasm that may take the homeopath months or even years to heal; as cure takes place different 'disease pictures' come up, so different remedies will be needed. Homeopathic medicine strengthens the whole system, and should gradually decrease your susceptibility to certain disorders. It will lessen the effect of inherited weakness, whatever it may be – we don't all have the same miasm to deal with – and over several generations it will improve vitality.

### The vital force

The concept of an invisible, yet tangible, 'vital force' is an ancient one. The Chinese call it *Chi*; the Indians, *Prana*. It is one of the cornerstones of homeopathic practice. The Renaissance alchemist, Paracelsus, believed that energy radiated between people – even acting at a distance when people were especially close emotionally. Many ancient cultures share a belief in some kind of animating spirit, soul or energy whose function is to give us consciousness, creativity and spiritual inspiration. The vital force is that mysterious agent which causes a seed to grow into a tree, a fertilized ovum into a human being, and which departs at

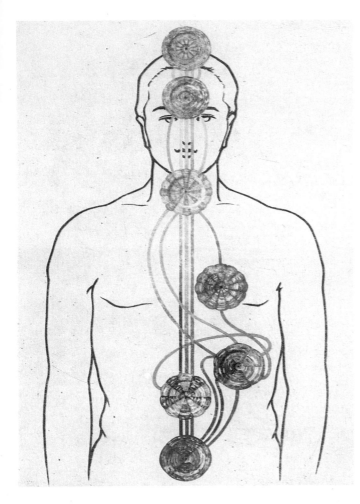

*Hindu and Buddhist religions regard the physical body as an interconnecting system of psychic energy centres called 'cakras' or 'chakras' (from the Sanskrit word for 'wheel'). There are many such energy centres in the body, of which seven are considered to be the most important. These are located in the major body plexuses, the junctions where several nerve networks meet. Cakras are controlled by Yoga techniques, which can be used to raise the potent energy stored in the lowest cakra at the base of the spine to the highest, at the top of the skull.*

death. By stimulating this life force when the body is sick, holistic therapies seek to encourage our innate healing energies to do their job. Indeed, homeopaths and others argue that an imbalance of this vital force is a fundamental cause of illness – for when the mental and emotional planes are disturbed, physical disease is not far away.

## Scientific evidence

In 1939 Semyon and Valentina Kirlian discovered a photographic technique which provided intriguing visual evidence of the vital force. By placing a living object, such as a freshly-picked leaf, on colour film in between two high voltage electrodes they were able to produce stunning, thought-provoking photographs. These Kirlian pictures showed a multi-coloured glow surrounding living things, remarkably similar to religious paintings depicting haloes around the heads of saints and angels. And further work revealed that this energy field was not a static phenomenon – it reflected changes in the mood and health of the subject.

Recent advances in Kirlian photography have increased its accuracy, although it is still regarded with suspicion by many scientists. However, American researcher L. W. Konikiewicz has refined the method considerably and is able to identify sex, the moment of ovulation, and the exact point of the menstrual cycle simply by looking at Kirlian photographs of unidentified finger prints.

*A Kirlian photograph of the hand. Kirlian photography (also known as electro-photography or radiation photography) uses no external light source. The bright image is the result of high energy interchange between the subject and an applied electrical field. The image indicates the correlation between mental and physical activity and the sweat rate and the composition of sweat on the surface of the skin.*

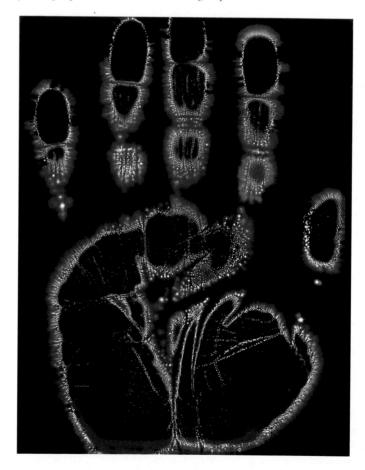

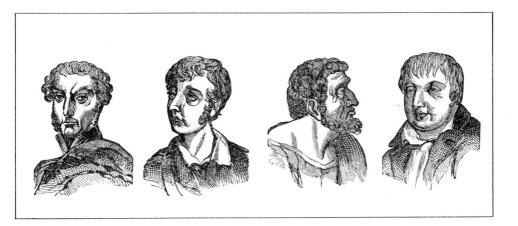

As scientific research becomes increasingly subtle, we may soon have further evidence for the existence of this elusive energy. But as Albert Einstein once said, 'The most beautiful thing we can experience is the mysterious. It is the source of all true science.'

## Homeopathic personalities

Medieval physiology was based, to a large extent, upon the doctrine of humours. A Sanguine individual, for instance, had a florid complexion and an optimistic, ardent temperament – he was considered to be literally full of blood. A Choleric person, on the other hand, was thought to be irascible and full of bile. The four humours, or fluids, were supposed to determine temperament or disposition – plus the types of illness to which you might succumb. Despite the simplicity and inadequacy of this old idea, certain personality types do seem to be more prone to specific kinds of disease. Modern 'bodymind' therapies such as Bioenergetics and Rolfing, clinical psychology, and scientists investigating psychosomatic illness have all identified definite links between mind and body. Increasingly, the evidence suggests that our bodies do seem to shape themselves physically in response to different mental and emotional characteristics.

In homeopathy the structure of the psyche and the structure of the body are seen as a whole, for mind and matter are indivisible. Homeopathic diagnosis encompasses personality traits, behavioural patterns and diverse physical symptoms. Each homeopathic remedy, therefore, addresses itself

*Until the 17th century, medical science was based on the idea that the body was permeated by four humours. They were black bile, corresponding with earth, heart, dryness and the emotion of melancholy; blood, corresponding with air, heat, wetness and a sanguine temperament; yellow bile, corresponding with coldness, dryness, fire and a choleric or bilious (angry) temperament; and phlegm, which corresponded with water, coldness, wetness and a phlegmatic temperament. Perfect health was considered to be the perfect balance of all four humours, and disorders were thought to arise from imbalance.*

to the current mental state of the patient concerned.

### The individual approach

Descriptions of homeopathic remedies also include precise pathological symptoms, upon which your final prescription is based. *Nux vomica,* for example, is a useful remedy for the kind of splitting headache brought on by over-indulgence; the person needing it will be irritable, chilly, sensitive to noise and upset by wine and coffee at the same time as craving them. *Pulsatilla* is a more suitable headache cure for weepy people. Indeed, there are many commonly-prescribed homeopathic remedies for headaches – each presenting a different symptom picture. Hardly anybody goes through life needing only one cure. By paying close attention to individual kinds of pain and discomfort the homeopath gradually builds up a symptom picture, and is able to isolate the remedy appropriate for the current complaint.

### Homeopathy and psychology

As we have seen, homeopathy places considerable emphasis upon mental and emotional health. Psychological attitudes are often just as relevant as physical symptoms – even when prescribing for animals. Suppressing emotions can be just as dangerous as suppressing inflammation or a fever – for even on a simple level this can increase the likelihood of illness. How often do you hear such phrases as 'I'm sick of this', 'it's a pain in the neck' or 'this is one big headache'. Indeed frequently our bodies obediently respond to these statements, and produce real symptoms to match.

Fear, anxiety, depression and nervous tension drive many people to seek relief – often in the form of stimulants, tranquillizers and sleeping pills. But as we are beginning to realize, these chemicals create more problems than they solve. Commonly prescribed tranquillizers such as Valium are addictive, and only serve to mask underlying problems – not solve them. Homeopathic treatment can be a very effective alternative to conventional mood-altering drugs, and also works well with psychological counselling.

Homeopathy is also helpful in treating nicotine and alcohol addictions and drug abuse problems. The law of similars may clearly be seen operating here, for *Coffea* is given to 'coffee addicts', *Tabacum* for smokers, and *Avena sat.* (oats) is often used for the treatment of alcoholics. An American psychiatrist, Dr. Jack Cooper, found homeopathic medi-

*Cholera rampaged through London in the mid 19th century, entirely caused by appalling sanitary conditions. Cholera is contracted by eating food or drinking water contaminated by human excrement, and is highly infectious. Homeopathy had the best record of curing this virulent yet avoidable plague.*

cines invaluable in his work at New York's Westchester County Prison – where he dealt with problems of drug addiction and alcoholism among the prisoners. He also observed that during the time he was prescribing the remedies there were no suicides. Yet before he began to use them, and after he left his job, a number of inmates killed themselves each year.

## Homeopathy and infectious disease

Some of homeopathy's first major success stories happened long before the discovery of antibiotics in the 1940s. When a cholera epidemic struck London in 1854, the mortality rate at the London Homeopathic Hospital was far lower than at other hospitals in the city – 16.4 per cent as against 51.8 per cent. And in a similar epidemic in Cincinnati in 1849 only 3 per cent of homeopathic patients died, compared with 40 to 70 per cent of those who were treated by conventional methods.

## Antibiotics – for and against

Infectious disease is caused by bacteria or viruses. Allopathic doctors generally prescribe antibiotics for bacterial infections, but viral infections tend not to respond to them and are consequently becoming an increasing problem. Antibiotics have undoubtedly relieved much pain and suffering. However, their wholesale use can not only impair

*A micrograph of the intestinal bacteria* Escherichia coli, *one of the harmless bacteria that dwell in the human gut. Antibiotics can strip the gut of such bacteria, the function of which is to destroy much of the waste product in the food we eat. A course of antibiotics is often accompanied by a mild stomach upset because of the reduction in protective bacteria.*

the body's own immune system, but has also led to the development of resistant strains of bacteria which fail to respond to treatment. New antibiotics are constantly being researched to overcome this problem – there are now 300 kinds of penicillin, for example.

'*Bios*' means 'life'. Antibiotics were so named because they destroy bacterial life by removing harmful bacteria from our bodies. Unfortunately, they also remove the beneficial bacteria that live inside us all the time, weakening the body and ironically rendering it more susceptible to fresh infection. Three to five hundred species of bacteria live in the intestinal tract, weighing three to four pounds – and it is these intestinal flora which help us to absorb nutrients from our food. This is why an upset stomach is a common side-effect of antibiotic treatment. Homeopathic medicine avoids such problems, and while it usually takes longer to work, recurrent infection is less likely. Where antibiotics are necessary – for possibly dangerous infections – a homeopath can help you to recover from their effects, and work toward eradicating the underlying causes so that the infection does not recur.

### Viral infections

In 1985 the British Homeopathic Journal published the results of some research on the antiviral effect of homeopathic medicines against viruses that attack chicken embryos. Eight out of the ten remedies tested were remarkably effective, inhibiting viral growth by 50 to 100 per cent. Homeopathy works against viral infections in four ways:

- *by increasing resistance*
- *by treating acute symptoms*
- *by providing support during convalescence*
- *by treating the after-effects or sequelae, which often develop following orthodox treatment*

Homeopathic prevention of infection from epidemics – such as typhoid or cholera – is often achieved by the use of *nosodes*. A nosode is taken orally, and is prepared from the actual bacteria or virus which causes the infection. Other remedies, which produce similar symptoms to the disease, may be used both to prevent and treat infection. Measles, for instance, is usually treated with *Pulsatilla* in the later catarrhal stage - which is also a prophylactic (preventive

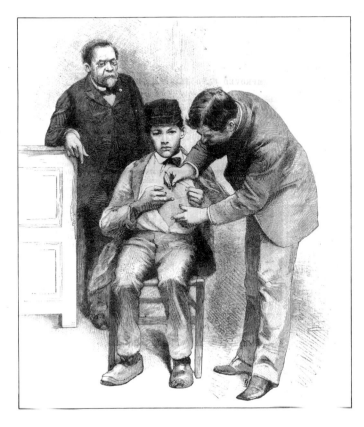

*Louis Pasteur (1822-1895) looks on as his assistant inoculates a shepherd boy who has been bitten by a rabid dog. Unfortunately, there is no record of the outcome of the exercise. Pasteur was not a homeopath; his method was to infect people with minute amounts of the same disease to which they had been exposed. Homeopathy prescribes a remedy which will induce the same symptoms as the disease, believing that the symptoms are indications of the body's fight to rid itself of the intruder. At the end of his life, Pasteur turned more to the homeopathic view.*

remedy) for this disease. How these two different types of remedy are prescribed is described more fully in Chapter 4.

Nosodes are also useful in the battle against whooping cough (*pertussis*), which sweeps through the population every four years or so. Some children cannot tolerate orthodox vaccine against this; homeopathic doses of the appropriate nosode offer a viable alternative for worried parents.

## Vaccination

Vaccination is often mistakenly thought to be 'homeopathic'; it isn't. Homeopathy cures like with like; vaccine offers 'the same' *not* something similar. Most homeopaths are opposed to vaccination in principle because it ignores the individual's state of health. It also prescribes the same dose indiscriminately. Some people may be susceptible to the disease being vaccinated against; others won't be. That is why people react very differently to vaccination. However, official regulations in many countries make it a condition of entry – but homeopathic treatment may be necessary to counteract the ill effects. Nosodes are available for most diseases; you can take them as a prophylactic before you go abroad and use repeat doses as necessary when you get to your destination.

### Treating after-effects

Many viral and bacterial illnesses leave people feeling at best exhausted, or at worst suffering a series of fresh infections or aches and pains. Sometimes the symptoms are so vague that they are rejected by conventional practitioners, or dismissed as hypochondria. Chronic after-effects may also be the result of vaccination, which can create a condition known as vaccinosis. In all these cases the appropriate nosode, relating to the original infection, is sometimes given to encourage and stimulate complete healing. Where

*Homeopathy is useful in sports injuries as it can effect a cure without the athlete suffering from the side-effects produced by powerful suppressant drugs supplied by orthodox medicine.*

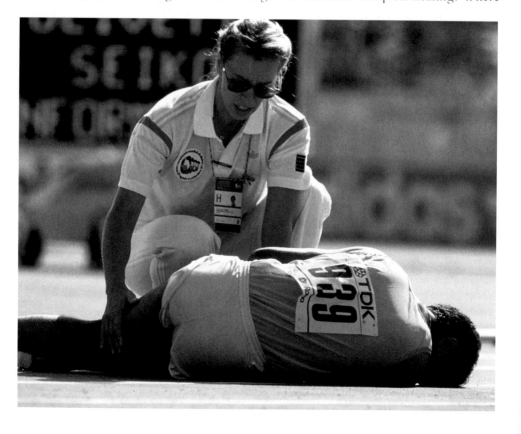

the virus has not been diagnosed, homeopathic remedies are individually prescribed as usual.

## Homeopathy and orthodox medicine

Homeopathy can be a very useful adjunct to orthodox treatment, and in many cases can replace it altogether. Dental problems, straightforward injuries, and post-operative healing all benefit from homeopathic treatment. It can also successfully deal with cysts and tumours, and in some cases removes the need for surgery.

Sports injuries are fairly simple to treat homeopathically, for a complex individual symptom picture is not usually required. Various Olympic athletes, including the 1984 British cycling team, have turned to homeopathy because they find that it works. *Arnica* ointment, for example, diminishes pain and speeds healing time considerably – and is used by many sports coaches and doctors as a result. Similarly, dentists are finding a number of homeopathic remedies very helpful in treating pain, inflammation and even hyper-sensitivity to amalgam fillings.

A common homeopathic saying is 'there are no incurable diseases, only incurable people'. Homeopathy, just like any other system of medicine, can fail to effect a cure for a number of reasons.

- *The patient may fail to give the doctor or practitioner sufficient information about himself, in which case it is human error that causes the problem, not homeopathy.*
- *The patient may already be beyond help – here homeopathy, like allopathy, can only hope to relieve fear and suffering as much as possible.*
- *Long-term use of conventional drugs creates side-effects, and these tend to obscure the true underlying symptoms. Epileptics and diabetics can be helped by homeopathy, but often cannot be taken off conventional medication immediately as their system would suffer from the shock of sudden withdrawal. In these cases, a homeopath would try to improve overall health.*

To the homeopath there is a healing process at work within the symptoms of every disease, but the process is different in each individual.

# 4

# HOW HOMEOPATHY WORKS

*Paracelsus (1493-1541), was an early promoter of the homeopathic principle. He announced that 'what makes a man ill also cures him', and went on to prove this by curing a village of the plague with medicine made with minute amounts of the villagers' own excreta.*

The principle that 'like cures like' is the cornerstone of the homeopathic approach to treatment. Associated with this principle are the use of the minimum effective dose of a remedy, the minimum repetition of the dose, and the minimum intervention in the process of healing.

Homeopathic remedies are different to conventional medication in strength, mixture, dosage and manufacture. It is just as important to understand how the remedies are made as it is to understand the principles of homeopathy.

### Preparing homeopathic remedies

Homeopathic medicines – or remedies, as homeopaths call them – are made from many substances. The preliminary treatment that each material needs to prepare it for the dynamizing process of dilution and succussion varies according to the substance. The original substance from which the remedy is to be made must be collected or otherwise prepared in the way that is as near as possible to the way it was done when preparing the material for proving.

Great care needs to be given to every detail of the process, so that the curative homeopathic properties are most accurately replicated. If this is not done, a new proving should be carried out in order to reveal any differences in effects caused by differences in preparation.

*Samual Hahnemann's remedy box, now the property of the Hahnemann Society. Many homeopaths keep their remedies in a box of this design, but few have one that is quite so splendid.*

## Tinctures

Once a plant, or part of a plant, has been gathered it is made into a tincture (called the 'mother tincture') in order to prepare it for potentization – the process of sequentially diluting the remedies to achieve higher and higher potencies. It is washed, and then the juice is extracted and added to absolute (water-free) alcohol.

The proportion of alcohol to juice varies with the plant and its condition, particularly the amount of water in the fresh plant; homeopaths have very specific criteria for this. This is how Hahnemann described the process of creating the original tincture, which we call mother tincture ($\Phi$):

> To utilize in the most complete and certain way the power
> of indigenous plants that can be obtained fresh, one
> thoroughly mixes the sap, immediately after it has been
> pressed out, with an equal amount of wine spirit strong
> enough for a sponge to burn in it. One then lets this stand
> for twenty-four hours in a tightly-closed bottle, and
> decants the clear liquid from the fibrous and albuminous
> matter that has settled, and stores it carefully for medicinal
> use. The wine spirit immediately stops all fermentation of
> the sap and makes subsequent fermentation impossible. By
> this method the medicinal strength of the sap can be
> permanently preserved, perfect and unspoiled, [and it can
> be] stored away from the sunlight in bottles that have been
> well closed with molten wax and sealed to prevent
> evaporation.

Recently a remedy has been made up from *Calendula officinalis*, the common marigold, with an interesting variation. A fresh tincture of the leaves and flowers is often used as a remedy for treating superficial cuts and grazes, and for treating other symptoms too. In this particular case the preparer deliberately chose a bloom growing near a busy highway, so that a remedy could be made that would be particularly suitable for the wounds of the modern city dweller. Strictly, a new proving of this remedy should also be done for the sake of accuracy.

When making up remedies from plants, the exact species must be carefully identified, and it is important to find the most perfect specimens of the species available. The plants should be collected in the optimum conditions, growing in their natural habitat. They should be harvested at a time when the part of the plant that is to be used is at its best, which is usually during spring or summer. The plants must be growing away from polluting factors, such as pesticides or artificial fertilizers leaching from nearby fields. Sadly, because so much of our atmosphere and water is polluted these days, it is difficult to ensure that there is no contamination. However, on the positive side, the fact that traces of some pollutants may be in the tinctures used for treatment may actually help people to fight off the effects of the environmental pollution that is now part of our every day lives.

### Trituration

The energetic properties of many minerals and other chemical substances, and even of some plant products, cannot be prepared for potentization by making tinctures because the materials are insoluble. The way they are prepared varies with each substance, but commonly the process involves what is called trituration: that is, grinding the substance with a specified amount of milk sugar, using a sterile pestle and mortar, for three hours. Milk sugar, also called lactose, is employed as a medium because of its neutral properties. This process reduces the remedy to the millionth dilution, also called 6x or 3C potency. At this level the substance is soluble in alcohol.

*Trituration is the process of grinding remedies that will not dissolve in alcohol together with milk sugar. After trituration, the mixture is soluble in alcohol.*

*Drop formation: a single drop of the mother tincture (made by dissolving the remedy in alcohol) is succussed (forcefully shaken) in various volumes of water or alcohol to make up the various potencies.*

## Making the potencies – dilution and succussion

There are two different ways of making each dilution before succussion.

The Hahnemannian method is to take one drop of the previous potency and dilute it with alcohol or double-distilled water in the specified proportion. It is then succussed. For the preparation of the next potency a fresh sterile phial is used.

In the Korsakoff method, after the succussion of the first potency the contents of the phial are poured off, either into another sterile container if the potency is to be kept, or down the drain if it is to be thrown away. One drop of the remedy is left clinging to the wall of the phial. Then fresh alcohol or distilled water is added 9, 99 or 49,999 drops according to the scale being used. In this method the same container is used for the making of each potency, except that from time to time a fresh sterile phial is taken to ensure contamination from the atmosphere is avoided. In the Korsakoff method 4, 6 or 8 phials may be used to make a 30 or 200 potency, whereas in the Hahnemannian method 30 or 200 phials are needed.

Hahnemann used pure alcohol with each new potency. This meant that to produce a high potency, tens of gallons of alcohol were needed. In practice this is very expensive, especially if the pharmacist is using the Hahnemannian method of dilution with a new phial each time. So today many pharmacies use double-distilled water for the intermediate potencies, and alcohol only for those they are going to keep. Many of the dilutions are not used, as experience has shown that certain potencies are the most effective.

*Succussion is the continued shaking of one drop of the mother tincture in a volume of neutral liquid (distilled water or alcohol). A drop of the resultant liquid can then be further succussed to make different potencies of remedy. Succussion may be done by hand or machine, but many homeopaths prefer the hand method.*

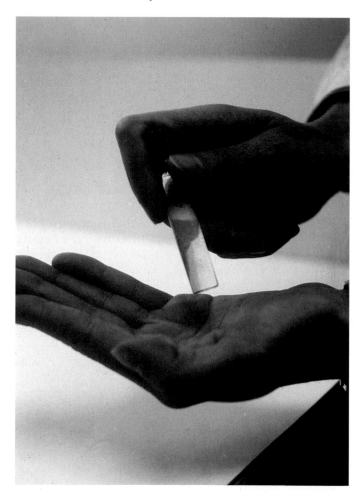

There is some disagreement about the validity of the Korsakoff method, but as there is no difference in the proportion of the dilution at each stage, there seems no scientific reason to doubt it. All these matters of debate in homeopathy, which turn on such infinitesimal measurements, may be clarified in the next few years as ever more accurate scientific measuring devices and experiments enable the action of remedies on human cells to be observed and properly interpreted.

## Succussion
Succussion, or forceful shaking, was originally done by hand. Nowadays much of it is carried out by machine, but even with mechanical aids it may take up to 10 or 12 weeks to prepare tinctures of the highest potencies. In the nineteenth century this time element led to the work of preparing some of these potencies being entrusted to people like lighthouse keepers, who had long, lonely hours on duty with only their light to tend. The rhythmic, carefully repeated motions required in trituration and succussion helped to keep them awake, while at the same time benefiting homeopathy.

Each succussion should be equivalent to the force exerted by an average healthy man when striking a hand-held phial (a firmly-stoppered test-tube or other laboratory container) forcefully against a firm surface. Hahnemann used a large leather-bound book. At each succussion the phial came to a brief stop, inertia making the liquid jump in the phial. Today machines imitate this action, but they need careful regulating and frequent maintenance to ensure that the succussion is standardized.

## What is potency?
Homeopathic potencies indicate the strength of remedies. The more a medicine is diluted the higher is its potency. The potencies are measured according to two principal scales of dilution – decimal and centesimal. In the *decimal scale* the potencies are diluted ten times each time. Such potencies are indicated by a number for the potency followed by the letter x in Britain and America (the letter D is used in Continental Europe); for example 6x or 6D. In the *centesimal scale* the potencies are diluted 100 times each time. Such potencies are indicated by a number for the potency followed by the letter C in Britain and America (CH in Continental Europe); for example 6C or 6CH.

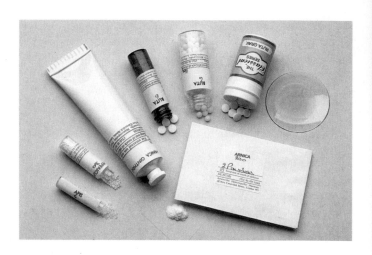

*Homeopathic remedies look much like allopathic ones. Here you can see (left to right) granules, pilules, ointment, small tablets, large tablets, tincture and powder. Apart from the tinctures, homeopathic remedies generally have a mild sweet taste.*

Remedies may be prepared for use in the form of tinctures (alcohol-based liquids), pilules, tablets, triturations, granules or powders. Whichever form is used, it is labelled with the potency according to either the decimal or the centesimal scale, more rarely with the Greek letter *phi* ($\Phi$)signifying mother tincture.

Hahnemann said that the method used in preparing the various potencies played an important part in releasing the energetic quality of the substances used. From the initial mother tincture or trituration one drop or grain of it is diluted or triturated with 9 or 99 or 49,999 drops or grains of alcohol or lactose, The resulting dilution is succussed in a specific way between 40 and 100 times, whatever the pharmacist decides. This succussion makes the first decimal, first centesimal or first millesimal (see page 54) potency.

### What is left?

From this it will be seen that the amount of the original remedy left in the higher potencies is very small indeed. Scientists use a quantity known as a mole to measure chemical substances. One mole contains 602,252 million million million particles, atoms or molecules (written as $6.02252\times10^{23}$). This number is called Avogadro's number (after the Italian scientist Amedeo Avogadro, a contemporary of Hahnemann). It corresponds in dilution to 24x or 12C or 6LM. From this it would seem that potencies higher than those will no longer contain even a single molecule of the original remedy.

### A scientific explanation?

But perhaps we are now on the verge of a more positive modern scientific explanation of the working of homeopathy. New theories in physics and biochemistry are being refined to a point where it may be possible to explain homeopathy in scientific language. They talk of energies and particles of microscopic and sub-microscopic 'life' which are found in everything. These seem to resemble what Hahnemann called *Lebenskraft*, which may be translated as 'vitality', or as many English-speaking homeopaths call it, 'vital force'. According to these new theories, it would seem that the process of dilution and succussion (shaking) by which the remedies are prepared releases the basic particle structure of the curative substance into the medium with which it is diluted. Therefore, the curative effect of the remedy is through the energy field of the substance matching the energy field of the disordered system. In this way the homeopathic remedy stimulates the vital force.

In 1984 Paul Callanin, an Australian biophysicist, gave a lecture to the Institute for Complementary Medicine in London at which he showed electron microscope photographs of frozen crystals of homeopathic remedies at various potencies. These pictures, taken with polarized light, showed that the same remedy in different potencies had different crystal patterns. Callanin took the photographs in the course of research aimed at proving the action of homeopathic remedies through the water bridges affecting the globular proteins in enzymes, thus affecting cellular function. He considered that certain potencies worked best because the structural pattern of the remedy was stronger at some potencies than at others, and these potencies were the most likely to affect the water bridges.

The mathematician David Bohm in his book *Wholeness and the Implicate Order* talks about the assumption that within any energy system there seems to be an inherent desire for order. So when a disorder appears, the system struggles to get rid of whatever is causing the disorder. When a homeopathic remedy is given it rids the system of disorder, and thereby re-establishes order within the body.

If you consider the human organism as being like a radio receiver, and the remedy required as radio waves reaching that receiver then you will see it is appropriate that with homeopathic remedies the medicine of the right 'wavelength' is chosen – in other words, the right potency. So for some diseases of a purely physical nature you would need a 'long-wavelength' potency, in other words a low potency; for some deep-seated disorders with a mental or emotional element a 'short-wavelength' remedy, that is a high potency, would be appropriate.

### Development of the potency scales

The potency scale preferred by Hahnemann, and by many other homeopaths who follow his teaching closely, is the centesimal. Each centesimal potency is equivalent in dilution to two decimal potencies; in other words 30C potency is the same dilution as 60x. However, the 60x will have received twice as many succussions, and is therefore regarded as a higher potency (potencies in the decimal scale above 60x are seldom used). It is the process of succussion which releases the dynamic energy of each dilution into the solvent.

It is not yet known what degree of difference this really makes to the action of the remedy in respect of analyzed statistics from clinical comparisons, but mathematically there is a difference. Choosing the right potency for a patient does follow some general rules, but is also a matter for the judgement of the practitioner, based on clinical experience.

The *millesimal* (LM) *scale*. diluting the remedy by 1 part to 49,999 for each potency, was developed by Hahnemann towards the end of his life. However, this was not known until the sixth edition of Hahnemann's *Organon* was discovered in this century and was then translated and published in the United States in 1921 by Dr William Boericke, first Professor of Homeopathic Materia Medica and Therapeutics at the University of California.

### Hahnemann's followers

After Hahnemann's death, his followers went on to develop and use higher potencies themselves. The so-called high-potency prescribers of today in practise use any potency, from 1x or even mother tincture to the highest, depending on the needs of the patient, repeating the doses only as needed, and changing to a high or low potency according to the patient's reaction to the remedy.

Hahnemann does not seem to have used anything higher than the 200C potency until he developed the millesimal potencies in his later years.

| POTENCIES AND THEIR DILUTIONS | | | | | |
|---|---|---|---|---|---|
| **DECIMAL SCALE** | | **CONTINENTAL SCALE** | | **50 MILLESIMAL/LM SCALE** | |
| **Potency** | **Dilution** | **Potency** | **Dilution** | **Potency** | **Dilution** |
| 1X | $\dfrac{1}{10}$ | 1C | $\dfrac{1}{10^2}$ | 1m | $\dfrac{1}{50 \times 10^4}$ |
| 2X | $\dfrac{1}{10^2}$ | 2C | $\dfrac{1}{10^4}$ | 2m | $\dfrac{1}{2 \cdot 5 \times 10^9}$ |
| 3X | $\dfrac{1}{10^3}$ | 3C | $\dfrac{1}{10^6}$ | 3m | $\dfrac{1}{1 \cdot 25 \times 10^{14}}$ |
| 6X | $\dfrac{1}{10^6}$ | 6C | $\dfrac{1}{10^{12}}$ | 6m | $\dfrac{1}{1 \cdot 5 \times 10^{28}}$ |
| 9X | $\dfrac{1}{10^9}$ | 7C | $\dfrac{1}{10^{18}}$ | 30m | $\dfrac{1}{9 \times 10^{136}}$ |
| 12X | $\dfrac{1}{10^{12}}$ | 12C | $\dfrac{1}{10^{24}}$ | 200m | $\dfrac{1}{9 \times 10^{919}}$ |

Hahnemann considered that the pharmacist preparing homeopathic remedies should also be a homeopathic practitioner, and should give a great deal of thought to the ideal image of the substance and its remedy picture, especially during the preparation of the mother tincture and the first potencies. This makes sense in the light of recent investigations into the ways that the unconscious thoughts and intentions of experimenters can influence experiments.

In support of this precept of Hahnemann's is the observation made recently that remedies that have been prepared by hand by practising homeopaths seem to be more dynamic in their action – even in lower potencies – than machine-made potencies.

### Clinical use of potencies

From clinical experience, practitioners have found that different scales of potency seem to be more effective than others for certain conditions. The different potencies within each scale may suit some patients or their conditions better than others.

The harmonic progression of potencies that Hahnemann used was 3C, 6C, 9C, 12C, 15C, 18C, and so on. This progression seems to be particularly effective in treating people suffering from major chronic physical diseases who have a low vitality. It seems that in severe acute conditions, if the vital force is good and the indications clear, high potencies work best. This is not always true, however, as a recent research project, despite being poorly analyzed statistically, demonstrated. It indicated that bruises responded better to the higher dilution of *Arnica montana* 10M (1,000C) than the lower dilution of 30C.

A different progression seems to be especially useful in the treatment of functional, psychosomatic and mental disorders. It was developed by an American homeopath, Dr James Tyler Kent, who taught and practised in Chicago in the nineteenth century. He produced the most comprehensive repertory, *Repertory of the Homeopathic Materia Medica*, but he died before the publication of the sixth edition of Hahnemann's *Organon* and the millesimal scale. Kent's scale is 6C, 12C, 30C, 200C, 1,000C, 10,000C, 50,000C, and so on (from 1,000C upwards the Roman numeral M is used for convenience to indicate thousands of centesimals, as 1M, 10M, 50M; this should not be confused with the small m used to denote potencies in the millesimal (LM) (scale).

## Taking the remedies

A quantity of a potentized remedy, once made, lasts a long time if it is preserved in the appropriate conditions, without exposure to direct sunlight and heat, strong odours or other contaminants. It goes a long way because such a small amount of the remedy is used. One dose consists of one drop of tincture, placed under the tongue, put into a little water and sipped, or put on a tablet made from milk sugar, which is then dissolved in the mouth. Remedies can be made up by the pharmacist – by mixing tincture with milk sugar, which is then placed in moulds like miniature patty pans to set and dry; this method makes soft, melt-in-the-mouth tablets.

Some practitioners prefer to administer tincture rather than tablets so that they can be sure an adequate amount of the remedy has been given, to be absorbed through the mucous surfaces of the mouth. A remedy can be administered by olfaction, that is inhaling the vapour emanating from a bottle of the tincture, thus absorbing the action of the remedy through the mucous surface of the nose. If a patient is unconscious, a remedy can safely be placed under the tongue, or just inside the lower lip.

*Homeopathic remedies are most effective when they are dissolved on the tongue. If a disease picture indicates a complicated programme of remedies is required, the homeopath prefers to administer them himself. Remedies are best taken at least half an hour after a meal, and it is important to avoid all coffee (real or decaffeinated) while taking homeopathic remedies, as it can distort the disease picture.*

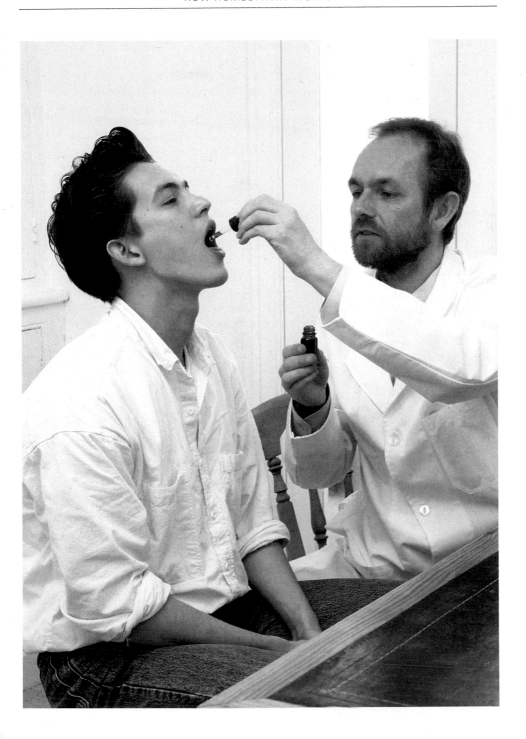

## SOME HOMEOPATHIC MATERIALS

*Those who are particularly interested in homeopathic pharmacy will know the* Homeopathic Pharmacopoeia of the United States *(sixth edition, revised, Clapp and Son, Boston, 1941), which is considered to be the most definitive work of its kind. Additionally, Indian homeopaths have proved some Indian herbs which are not yet included in the standard works, while O A Julian of France has proved some of the modern drugs such as penicillin and the major tranquillizer chlorpromazine (also called Largactil). To give an idea of the scope of the materials, without going into too much botanical or chemical detail, here is a short selection:*

**Aconitum** (common aconite, *Aconitum napellus,* also known as monk's hood and wolf's bane; extremely poisonous; grows in pastures and wastes of mountainous regions in southern and central Europe, Russia, Scandinavia and central Asia). As *n.o. ranunculaceae,* tincture of the whole plant with root made when it is just about to flower.

**Baryta carbonica** (barium carbonate, $BaCO_3$, with which are included symptoms of *Baryta acetica,* barium acetate, $BA(C_2H_3O_2)_2$).
The carbonate is used as a triturate; the acetate in solution. Symptoms include retarded growth in children, debilitating fatigue and numbness.

**Chininum arsenicosum** (arsenate of quinine ($C_{20}OH_{24}N_2O_2$) $_3H_3AsO_4.2H_2O$).
Used as a triturate or a solution. Symptoms include anorexia and continuous fever.

**Crotalus horridus** (the rattlesnake of North America).
Symptoms of the South American species *Crotalus durissus* are included in the proving. A trituration is made with sugar of milk (lactose) saturated with the venom, and a solution of the venom is made with glycerine. Symptoms include nervous shock, septic and malignant conditions.

**Flammula jovis** (clematis, Virgin's Bower *Clematis erecta*).
As *n.o. ranunculaceae* tincture of the leaves and stem; a
remedy for eye, skin and genital infections.

**Iodum** (tincture of iodine). This has a particular affinity for the
throat, chest and digestion, and is also prescribed for liver
infection and jaundice.

**Psorinum** (the nosode of psora, or scabies vesicle).
The sero-purulent matter of a scabies vesicle was used by
Hahnemann; the product of *Psora sicca* by Gross; and the
salt from a product of psora by Constantine Hering.
Triturations of all three are used.

**Rumex crispus** (curled dock, family Polygonaceae).
A tincture is prepared from the fresh root. Symptoms include
neuralgia and persistent tickling coughs.

**Sulphur** (brimstone, sublimated sulphur, S). A trituration is
prepared from flowers of sulphur, while a saturated solution
of sulphur in absolute alcohol constitutes the mother tincture.
A trituration of amorphous sulphur has also been used. The
effects of 'Milk of Sulphur', or precipitated sulphur, are
included in the pathogenesis (origin, development and
effects of a disease). Sulphur is discussed in detail on page 65.

**Tabacum** (tobacco, *Nicotiana tabacum,* family Solanaceae).
A tincture is prepared from the leaves before the flowers
develop. Symptoms include constricted muscles in the throat
and chest, vertigo, and convulsions.

**Tarantula hispania,** made by asphyxiating the tarantula spider
and placing it in alcohol.
As *n.o. araeida* tincture of spider it is indicated for mania,
hyperactivity, and chorea as well as septic outbreaks.

Most classical homeopathic practitioners use the centesimal scale of potencies, although a few use the millesimal. Some Indian practitioners have a great deal of experience in the use of these LM potencies.

Doses of the low decimal potencies, and the LM potencies, are intended to be repeated much more often than the potencies in the centesimal scale. Some practitioners repeat higher centesimal potencies in the same way, possibly having misinterpreted what Hahnemann wrote about the use of the LM potencies. Among them is Dr Francisco Eizayaga of Argentina. He thinks that there can be no harm in repeating doses of potencies on the centesimal scale because the patient, once the remedy has started to act, is no longer susceptible to the action of further doses; such doses act as placebos until the patient once again needs the action of the remedy, when the doses automatically become effective once more.

When the body needs the remedy it responds to it; when it does not need it, it ignores it. Many practitioners disagree with this approach, fearing that strong aggravations may be created in this way, but it certainly seems to work for Dr Eizayaga's patients.

### Ten types of prescriptions

There are ten main types of prescriptions. Unless otherwise indicated, all doses are to be taken on or under the tongue, not swallowed. They should be taken well away from the time that any other substance has been (or will be) in the mouth – such as food, drink, or toothpaste – an hour afterwards or 30 minutes before. This avoids any such substance interfering with the remedy. A good time to take an important constitutional remedy is either in the evening, well away from supper or brushing the teeth, so that it can start its healing action at the time when the body is normally giving time to resting and repairing itself; or first thing in the morning after the mouth has been rinsed with clear water, so that any symptoms of change can be observed.

**The single homeopathic dose** One drop of tincture or two tablets at one time. The single dose tends to be used with the higher potencies and in chronic conditions. It is then not followed up for four to six weeks. This is the traditional model of James Tyler Kent, which has been further developed during the twentieth century by homeopaths

George Vithoulkas of Greece and Joseph Reves of Israel. It has many virtues. A deeply perceptive understanding of the process of cure in the individual is needed by the practitioner in order to obtain the optimal results from this method, which often seem miraculous. But there are times when other forms of prescribing are needed.

**The collective single dose** Repeated dosing with the same potency of the remedy, given within a few hours. This is usually done with medium to high potencies, mainly to ensure that the remedy has acted. Some practitioners consider that this is pushing the action of the remedy too strongly, but this type of prescribing is often needed at the start of an acute condition.

**A split dose** Two doses of the same potency given within twelve hours, usually last thing at night and first thing in the morning. This method is useful in chronic conditions when the patient's vitality needs boosting. Again, this dosing is done with the higher potencies.

**The single cumulative dose** Repeated doses of higher potencies until some reaction is observed, or signs and symptoms of aggravation set in. Close observation by a practitioner and a perceptive patient is needed in this method. It may be useful in acute or serious flare-ups of chronic conditions, especially in hospitals and clinics.

**The ascending collective dose** Three doses of a remedy of successively higher potency within James Kent's progression of the centesimal potencies, for example, 12C, 30C, 200C, or 30C, 200C, 1M. These are given at intervals within a 12- or 24-hour period. This method reduces the likelihood of aggravation in some cases.

**Repeated low potencies followed by a complementary remedy in a high potency** Useful when the patient is known to have a weakness of a specific organ. The low potency remedy is a 'drainage' remedy aimed at strengthening and detoxifying the affected organ before a stronger, more individually constitutional remedy is given. However, the drainage remedy should be relevant to the particular signs and symptoms displayed by the patient, connected with the organ that is being strengthened.

***A high potency given before the repeated use of a low potency complementary remedy*** It is more difficult here to analyze what is doing what. This system of prescription may be needed for patients who are already on a course of allopathic drugs which they cannot be suddenly taken off. It is helpful to detoxify the system of patients who have previously had a lot of medication, or have been addicted to alcohol or drugs. The higher potency may also need repeating more often than is usual in these circumstances because of the depressing effect of some allopathic medication on the vital energy.

This system is also useful in treating elderly patients, but with them the high potency should not be too high, because the vitality of the elderly may not be strong enough to cope with the dynamic action of a very high potency. It is specifically useful in heart conditions, reduced liver and kidney activity, diabetics and severe gross pathological conditions. Repeated doses of a low potency drainage remedy may be useful for patients who cannot accept the idea that they only need one dose of medicine, and may also reduce any aggravations. This method was favoured by the late Dr Margery Blackie, homeopathic physician to Her Majesty Queen Elizabeth II.

***A single high dose; if no reaction repeat until there is a reaction, then stop*** This method of prescription is most useful in acute cases. It can also help in some chronic cases where a positive reaction is needed within hours or at the most days.

***Repeated doses of millesimal potencies*** These are meant to be repeated three of four times a day for days or even weeks; unless there is an aggravation, when repetition is stopped until the aggravation subsides. Then if necessary the remedy is resumed. Repetition is resumed until there is sufficient improvement to warrant the treatment being stopped.

***Daily repetition of decimal or low centesimal potencies*** Can be useful in some chronic conditions, especially if the patient is not strong. As with the LM potencies, the repetition should be temporarily stopped and the case reassessed if there is any aggravation of signs and symptoms. This dosing needs constant monitoring.

## Timing of remedies

There are some other points about the timing of remedies and when they should be administered. In women particularly it can be important to give a constitutionally-prescribed remedy away from the time of menstruation. In amenorrhoea (absence of menstruation) a high potency remedy is best given before the expected date of the next period.

For complaints which appear or are aggravated at certain times of the year, such as the seasonal complaint hay fever, a remedy should be given one or two months before the trouble is expected to start. The remedy should fit the chronic symptom picture, including all aspects of the patient's health picture.

For functional conditions, it may be worth giving the remedy one or two hours before the normal daily time at which the patient's signs and symptoms appear.

For epilepsy no medication is given during a convulsion, but it is administered afterwards.

Constitutional remedies are often very effective if they are given at the end of an acute illness, when the patient's vital force has been making a great effort to throw toxic elements to the surface from the deeper organs, and restore a better level of health.

## Experiment and dissension

Hahnemann was trained as a chemist as well as a physician. So he brought good chemical background to his experiments. As time went on he experimented with higher and higher dilutions, culminating in the millesimal scale. He found that the higher potencies became more and more dynamic in their therapeutic action, and often produced less aggravation of signs and symptoms in the healing process. Hahnemann was a devout Christian, and it may be that his strong belief in God and the power of the spirit enabled him to leap in his thinking beyond the purely materialistic approach to chemistry that was being developed in his day, and which persists in some instances today.

When Hahnemann began experimenting with these very high potencies, some of his followers who had a strongly materialistic view of science and rational schools of thought found it difficult or impossible to believe that the remedies would work. This was the argument that many allopathic doctors used, and still use to this day.

Consequently a division arose between the 'materialist' physicians in homeopathic practice, and the 'dynamists' who followed Hahnemann.

The materialists used only the lower range of potencies, and tended to mix several remedies together as herbalists do. They broke away from Hahnemann, and rejected many of his principles in respect of the ideas of disease and cure. They tended to adopt an allopathic approach to the use of homeopathic remedies, often giving several different potencies of remedies at the same time, with frequent repetitions of doses. They prescribed remedies for specific organs, concentrating on what they called 'drainage'. The countries where this method of prescribing is most used today are France, Germany, Italy and Switzerland.

It is interesting to note that it was the low-potency prescribers who were most willing to join with the American Medical Association in the late nineteenth century, thereby encouraging the suppression of homeopathy in the United States. Classical homeopathic prescribers around the world are determined that such suppression will not occur again, in any country.

## How the principles work in practice

A homeopathic practitioner views your signs and symptoms not just as the expression of disease, but as an indication of your body's own attempts to heal itself. So the practitioner seeks to find a medicine that stimulates a process that is already going on, one which follows through and works with the body's own defence mechanisms, resulting in the reduction of the signs and symptoms. On the principle of 'like cures like', the homeopath selects a remedy which, taken in an allopathic dose, appears to most closely resemble the patient's signs and symptoms.

For example, if you are suffering from the type of influenza that produces aching joints, aching bones, hot and cold shivers, nausea and vomiting of bile, coupled with a desire for cold drinks, then the homeopath will look for a medicine which could produce a similar 'symptom picture' in a healthy person. In this case the practitioner would be most likely to select *Eupatorium perfoliatum*, which is prepared from a North American plant of the daisy family, whose popular names are thoroughwort, feverwort and boneset. The primary characteristic symptoms of *Eupatorium perfoliatum* are aching pains and biliousness.

## A case for *Sulphur*

As a further example, consider a case history, which demonstrates how the signs and symptoms are noted and analyzed in great detail.

The patient is a man aged 60, with a history of digestive and skin troubles since childhood. As a child he had appendicitis, and as an adult a spastic colon and diverticulosis. He now suffers from early-morning digestive disturbances, acid regurgitation and burping.

The patient has a particular liking for meat, fish, cheese, bread, butter and savoury foods. His strong desire for beer and wine verges on alcoholism, and he drinks at lunchtime and in the evenings everyday. When he comes for consultations he often smells strongly of drink. The skin troubles he has had are urticaria (nettle rash) as a child; acne in adolescence; a series of boils in the groin, in the armpits and on the legs in his twenties, followed by the development of psoriasis (a common chronic itching skin disease which usually affects the elbows, knees and back). He now has a continual itching rash, particularly on his legs. He also suffers from post-nasal catarrh, which again is worse in the morning.

He is a warm-blooded person, with a ruddy complexion, and he easily becomes sweaty and over-heated. He gets dizzy on rising in the mornings, and has a slight loss of hearing, particularly of high frequencies. Last year he had an anxious time because of his wife's ill-health and his own early retirement.

In analyzing this case the practitioner has to consider that the remedy chosen must – besides fitting all the individual signs and symptoms – have a particular affinity with the digestive system and the liver and skin, because these appear to be the organs principally affected. The remedy which was prescribed, and produced an improvement in the patient, was *Sulphur*. This patient corresponds to the homeopathic drug picture for *Sulphur,* a classic case of someone who has done a lot of mental work all his life, has not taken much exercise, has done well at his profession, and has quite a high degree of self-confidence. He has abused his digestive and circulatory systems, which is shown by the red distended veins on his face and legs, and has a desire for a lot of fatty food as well as alcohol. His system has reacted by producing skin eruptions and digestive disturbances.

The level of disease in this case is not particularly deep. The main cause for concern is his desire for alcohol, which partly results from his lifestyle. Overall, he does not have many strong or emotional signs and symptoms. His concentration is good and, although retired, he is leading a very active life – becoming involved with his community and continuing to exercise his mind by attending adult education classes.

## Hahnemann and *Sulphur*

Hahnemann originally discovered the homeopathic use of sulphur by observing two of its characteristics. Firstly sulphuric ointment was traditionally used for the treatment of skin rashes, but when used in this way it produced other symptoms, such as abnormal appetite. Secondly, he noticed that skin eruptions and digestive troubles were common in people who lived in areas where there was a lot of sulphur in the water, such as the spa town of Baden–Baden in Germany, a popular and fashionable watering-place in the nineteenth century.

The leading twentieth century British homeopath Dr John Henry Clarke has this to say about sulphur in his *Materia Medica:*

> *As early as two thousand years ago, says Hahnemann, sulphur has been used as the most powerful specific against the itch; the itch with which the workers in wool are so much affected . . .. Sulphur frequently produces in healthy persons burning, itching pimples and vesicles resembling the itch vesicles, and especially itching in the joints and at night.*
>
> *Unfortunately the specific power of sulphur to cure the itch was much abused. It was applied externally as baths and ointments; as a result the skin affection [pathological condition] was not cured but repelled, and a host of secondary affections appeared in its place. Hahnemann found in sulphur the homeopathic counterpart of the peculiar constitutional [disorder] dyscrasia (abnormal physiological condition, principally of the blood) which tends to manifest itself in itch-like eruptions and which he named psora. Sulphur is the chief of the anti-psoric remedies . . . The domestic use of sulphur (in the familiar 'brimstone and treacle') as a 'spring medicine' is based on its anti-psoric properties.*

### *Coffea cruda*

Another example of a substance which produces signs and symptoms in its crude state, but cures similar signs and symptoms in homeopathic dilutions, is coffee (homeopathic remedy *Coffea cruda*, unroasted coffee). Coffee addicts often use this drink to keep themselves going late at night, or to stimulate the nervous system in order to keep on working when their bodies are wanting to rest.

Large quantities of coffee frequently produce keyed-up, excitable or irritable behaviour with changes of mood in people who are sensitive to its action. These people are also likely to find that immoderate coffee drinking affects their digestion. Sleeplessness may result because the mind has been overexcited, and the imagination is overflowing.

*Taking the waters in the sulphur bath at Kusatsu Onsen spa in Japan. Hahnemann used sulphur as an anti-psoric (anti-itch) remedy, but disapproved of unregulated external use.*

Therefore *Coffea* given in a homeopathic potency actually works towards relieving sleeplessness caused by over-activity of the mind; irritability and nervous tension; and the ill-effects of over stimulation of the nervous system. It can also relieve the digestive, urinary, respiratory, and heart symptoms that some people suffer from if they drink too much coffee – a substance which many of us regard as a normal part of our daily lives. This is an excellent example of the curative effect of a homeopathic remedy.

## Proving a remedy

Hahnemann's original discovery of the principle 'like cures like' – or the Law of Similars – came when he experimented on himself with Peruvian Bark (*Chinchona*), which produced in him all the symptoms of malaria. Since large doses of Peruvian Bark (a source of quinine) were then used with some success to cure malaria, Hahnemann realized that the standard medical approach of quelling symptoms with medicines that had an opposite effect might be wrong. He followed up his original observations, and experimented on his colleagues, friends and family as well as himself.

Extremely detailed notes were made on every possible symptom experienced by these pioneers. Hahnemann also conducted considerable medical library research, recording details of poisoning through the centuries that had been noted by numerous doctors in different countries. After six years of intensive experimentation and research, Hahnemann began to see patients once again – and could refer to 'proven' remedies and their symptoms for guidance.

## The minimum dose

But how do you administer a remedy that is similar in its effect to a patient's signs and symptoms if the substance which is being used as a remedy is in fact poisonous? This is another question that Samuel Hahnemann asked himself at the time he was developing his theories of homeopathy. To answer it, he experimented on himself, his family and his friends to find out what was the minimum amount of a substance that could be given to a person and still be curative.

By carrying out very careful preparations and observations, Hahnemann discovered that the more he diluted a substance – in a very precise way – the more effective it became in improving the health of a patient. As well as drastically reducing the fashionably large doses of his day, he was accomplishing a cure in a new way, by administering not a drug to counterpart the signs and symptoms, but one which would produce just those signs and symptoms if administered in a large dose. As a result of these early experiments, Hahnemann developed very exact formulae for the way in which homeopathic medicines should be prepared.

Because so little of the drug is present in the majority of homeopathic remedies in the potencies in which they are prescribed, people trained in Newtonian and Cartesian physics say that homeopathy must in fact be simply faith healing. They maintain that the remedies merely act as placebos, and patients feel better just because someone has taken the time to listen and talk to them about their troubles.

It is undoubtedly true that people's minds and wills can affect their bodies' ability to heal themselves. Evidence of this has come in recent years from studies of cancer sufferers carried out by an American team, Carl Simonton, an oncologist (a tumour specialist) and his wife Stephanie, a psychologist. In some cases placebos do effect cures, whatever treatment the patients have. But it is equally true that a homeopathic practitioner who gives an inappropriate remedy sees neither a real curative process going on in the patient nor the change in serious physical pathology which the correct remedy will stimulate.

## Choosing a remedy

A homeopathic practitioner tries to match your 'disease picture' most closely with an appropriate remedy which fits the complete picture of your disease signs and symptoms, not just individual signs and symptoms. The practitioner looks for the remedy that most closely fits all aspects of your problem, mental and emotional as well as physical. It is a rule in classical homeopathy to give only one remedy at a time; if the pattern of your disease picture changes as time goes on, then the practitioner changes the remedy to match the new picture.

Why is the term 'picture' used with respect to remedies and signs and symptoms? As you will have noticed from the case study of the man for whom *Sulphur* was prescribed, all the complaints from which he was suffering clearly showed some aspects of his personality as well as his disease; in addition his suffering showed some individual features. Taken together, all these details build up a complete picture of the patient in the mind of the practitioner. Over the years it has

**Proof at last?** The French Medical Research Council of Paris has come up with what is possibly the first piece of 'scientific' evidence to support one of the principles behind homeopathy. Professor J. Benveniste of the University of Paris-Sud, has been working with antibodies related to those that cause such allergic reactions as hayfever. He has found that molecules of the antibody were still active when diluted with distilled water, to the point where none of the antibody was left. Nothing is there, but the solution is biologically active, just as homeopathic remedies are. Professor Benveniste's experiments were replicated and repeated as double-blind trials, but the results were still the same.

Homeopaths find it ironic that 'proof' of their beliefs should come, albeit reluctantly, from orthodox research.

*Matching the remedy to the disease picture is the central principle of homeopathic medicine. To do this successfully, the homeopath has to take detailed notes of all the symptoms his patient describes and all the signs that the patient's body and behaviour indicate. Once the picture has been drawn, the relevant remedy can be prescribed.*

been found that not only do physical and ordinary pathological conditions show up in the provings of remedies, but that people who are most likely to be affected by a similar medicine, and be relieved by it, tend to have similar personality traits. These traits may be inherent, or have been built up or reinforced by upbringing, environment, and other influences. So we include that 'personality sketch' in the remedy picture.

What we are in effect doing is to match the personality found to go with a particular remedy to the personality of the patient that emerges while the initial examination is going on. This does not mean that we are trying to change the patient's personality, or that certain character traits are pathological, but that we are trying to establish how the negative aspects of that personality can create disharmony within the patient.

## OBSTACLES TO CURE

*This diagram shows the main factors that can hinder the healing process.*

poor living conditions

poor nutrition

destructive personal relationships

overwork

work environment

previous disease not fully cured

negative attitude

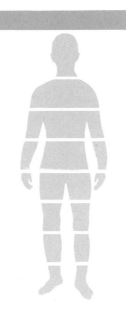

### Intervention and causes

Since homeopathic treatment emphasizes that all medication should be minimal, it follows that any other intervention should also be the least necessary to restore a patient to health. This includes the removal of any obstacles to cure, such as temporarily eliminating from the diet some food to which the patient may be allergic, or helping the patient to resolve some difficulties by counselling. For this reason, homeopaths consider surgery only when absolutely necessary; but it should be emphasized that homeopathy recognizes that there are cases for which an operation is essential.

The ill-effects of inoculations are sometimes an obstacle to cure. For example, it has been noticed that after the DPT (diptheria-pertussis-tetanus) triple vaccine commonly given in Britain, some children may develop chronic catarrhal problems, which are compounded by the use of antibiotics. Usually the homeopathic remedy most closely matching the drug picture seems to be most effective in treating the side effects, but in persistent cases a homeopathic potency of the disease product itself may be needed in order to clear the block to health created in the child's system. Inoculation side-effects may not present a picture for a single remedy, so for that problem a miasmic remedy may be prescribed.

*One of the factors damaging to good health is industrial pollution. This can affect us directly, through the air we breathe, or indirectly, through the food we eat. It is difficult to believe that the food produced from this cow, pastured in a field next to a chemical factory, will not be contaminated.*

## The effects of pollution

Today many people are subject to the effects of pollution in the atmosphere, in the water they drink and in the air they breath. Such pollution is frequently a major obstacle to cure. One of the commonest in people living in towns is the effect of lead on the system, most of it derived from the exhaust gases of cars. Lead has a general effect of slowing down the system and paralyzing it. It can find its way into the body through a variety of pathways; for example, air-borne lead from car exhausts can be deposited on growing crops, then washed into the soil and so leached into ground-water and the drinking water supply. Dr Robin Russell Jones, senior registrar at St John's Hospital, London, has written:

> *The average modern diet contains approximately 100 times as much lead as prehistoric diets. For water the ration is 750 times and for air the present-day ratio to pre-technological levels is a staggering 10,000 times.*

An Edinburgh University study of the effects of lead on the learning ability of children, published in *The Lancet* in 1987, concluded that in a group of Edinburgh children there was 'a significant relation between tests of ability and attainment . . . and blood lead when comfounding variables are taken into account.' An American study, published in *The New England Journal of Medicine* in 1987, concluded that prenatal exposure to lead had long-term effects, adversely affecting children's early learning.

Homeopaths are finding more and more often that the effects of lead and other heavy metals are bringing patients into their consulting rooms. Mercury and aluminium affect us all. For instance, mercury used in the amalgam for dental fillings can have disastrous consequences. Homeopathic *Mercurius* can be used to clear up some signs and symptoms resulting from such fillings, which affect some people quite strongly. One dentist, sensitive to mercury, was considering having to give up practice until she received homeopathic treatment. Another dentist gives patients homeopathic *Mercurius solubilis* if they are suffering from the ill-effects of mercury amalgam fillings; in extreme cases the fillings are replaced by modern porcelain or other non-metallic fillings. It is also interesting to note the decision made in 1987 by the Swedish Government Health Board, which declared amalgam toxic to be unsuitable as a dental filling material. Further, it planned to reduce and eventually ban the use of amalgam.

Aluminium is another metal that causes problems. It has strong effects on the system – affecting some people much more than others. It can get into food through the use of aluminium cooking ware, which is used both domestically and in the production of off-the-shelf foods. Recently it has been found that the brains of people suffering from Alzheimer's disease (a form of senile dementia suffered by those who have not yet reached old age) tend to contain quite a high proportion of aluminium. Aluminium is usually flushed out of the body via the kidneys.

However, homeopaths have known about the dangerous effects of some of these metals for quite a while, as can be seen from their provings of them. As a result of knowing the disease pictures of these metals, they have been able to prescribe for them when they see the signs manifested by their patients in the surgery, and so help people suffering from the effects of such pollutants.

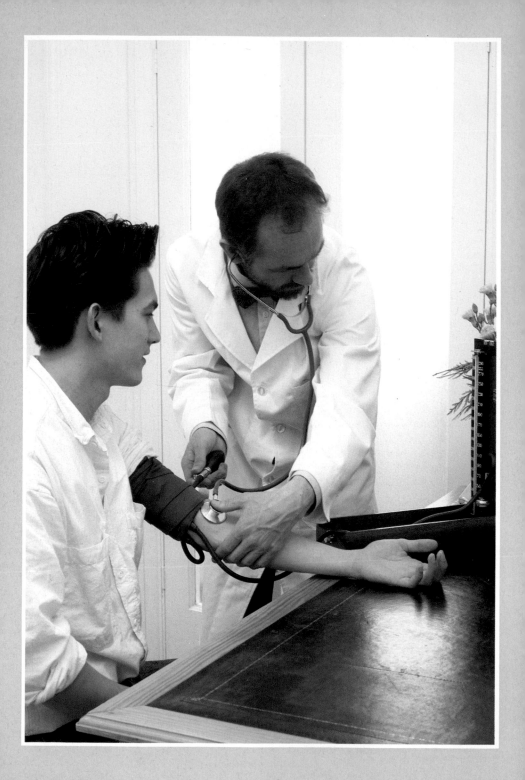

# 5

# HOMEOPATHY
# IN ACTION

Your decision to consult a homeopath could be the first step you make toward taking more personal responsibility for improving your health. Once you have made this commitment to yourself, you may wonder what to expect when you set out to visit a homeopath for the first time.

The first consultation may take from one to two hours. Be prepared to set aside enough time so that you can give your whole mind to the consultation without worrying about being late for another engagement. Because your homeopath will include many questions that you would not normally be asked by an allopathic practitioner, you would probably like to have some idea of the areas that will be covered.

*If you were going to change the world who would you start with, yourself or others?*

Alexander Solzhenitzyn

### What is happening now?

Most of the first questions put to you will be about whatever it is you have come for – that is, your current problem. Instead of wanting you to say 'I suffer from migraine' or 'I have a bad dose of flu' or 'I have menstrual pain', a homeopathic practitioner requires you to describe very specifically the way that you experience these conditions. So questions such as 'What sort of pain do you get with your migraine headaches?' are relevant. The homeopath needs to know which side of the head is affected; whether the headache is better when you lie down or when you walk about; what brings it on; whether it is worse as a result of eating certain foods or comes on after you have been angry; what happened when you first started getting headaches – was it during a period of stress in your life, or have you had any head injuries in your past?

Apart from all that, there may be other questions about what might, or might not, relieve the migraine headaches. Is it better for pressure, or the application of a cold flannel, or eating or not eating? The answers to all these very specific questions about the way you experience your headache are details the homeopath needs to know in order to find the best remedy for your complaint.

At the start of the consultation, tell the homeopath everything you have on your mind that you want help with. When you have done this, the practitioner will start asking questions in order to clarify specific details about the various symptoms. Once you have described all the details of your present problems, both chronic and acute – the homeopath will want details of your past medical history, which will

*When you visit a homeopath, much of the consultation will be taken up with talking. What your maternal grandfather did for a living, what kind of food you prefer, what times of day you feel better or worse, what kind of weather makes you feel better are all essential information if the homeopath is to draw up the correct disease picture, unique to you at the moment of consultation.*

give some idea how your present disease state may have developed. Questions will also be asked about the causes of possible past trauma, grief and illnesses, and the way they have been dealt with.

The homeopath will ask you about your family history, so before the consultation it would be useful to find out from relatives if they know of any chronic disorders or serious diseases or conditions that affected your parents and grandparents.

Perhaps you are going for a consultation with a physical disorder, such as rheumatism or asthma. However, the homeopath will ask questions about the way you interact with the world and other people; what sort of moods you have, whether you feel happy, irritable, depressed, angry, easily tearful or sad; whether your moods are changeable; whether you want to be with people or prefer to be on your own. Let the practitioner know whether or not you have

*Homeopaths measure blood pressure in the same way that orthodox medical practitioners do, and use the information to help them form the disease picture.*

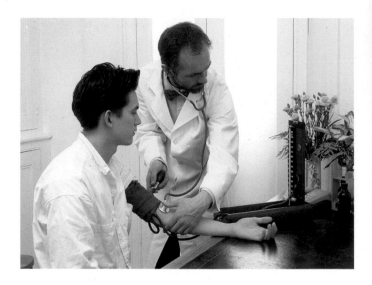

any irrational fears (phobias), or worries that prey on your mind, and tell him or her about stresses that you may have had in your life.

Even if they do not themselves define a disease, all of these details are relevant to finding the remedy picture that best fits you. Although such questions have less bearing on an acute condition, homeopathic practitioners are unlikely to accept you as a patient until they have taken your case history fully, in order to understand your constitution and its relationship with your current acute condition, and therefore your likely future treatment needs. This does not mean that homeopathy cannot treat acute conditions; it can. Indeed, some clinics will accept you for treatment for an acute condition without requiring a full consultation. But you might find subsequently that, if you want to go on using homeopathy as your form of medicine, you will need to follow up with a complete case history session. The homeopath will then become completely familiar with your case before any future treatment becomes necessary for acute conditions or disorders.

### Problems affecting the emotions

If you seem to be suffering from mostly emotional and mental problems, such as depression and loss of concentration, the homeopath will look upon those states as symptoms, and ask detailed questions about how you are expe-

riencing your particular moods. Such facts as when you feel
better, when you feel worse, and whether or not you are
sleeping well, are all important.

This interrogation may sound rather daunting, but be of
good heart. Homeopaths are used to talking with people
about their most intimate hopes and fears, and the more
willing you are to reveal information about your inner and
outer life, the more quickly and clearly the practitioner is
able to find the remedy required to help you to recover.

Other areas of your life that the homeopath may want to
elucidate (which may seem to you to be very trivial details)
include what foods you have an appetite for (not what you
*think* is good for you but what food and drinks you actually
desire), as well as the ones that you cannot stand. You, or
your individual signs and symptoms, may be sensitive to
temperature change; you may suffer in the heat and dry
weather of summer, or you may react badly to damp
weather or thunderstorms.

Further questions may be aimed at finding what seem to
be the causative factors of your current signs and symptoms. These may be connected with something you are
allergic to in your environment, such as industrial pollution. The causes may be associated with the break up of a
relationship, or sadness over the death of a relative. It is possible that the problems date back to a previous disease or
infection which was treated in a way that did not fully clear
its after-effects from your system, and weakened your constitution, so that as a result you have developed chronic
signs and symptoms. Some symptoms date back to an operation or an accident, after which you have never felt really
well.

It is clear from the experience of many patients that a large
proportion of people have chronic conditions which certainly stem from some difficult or unhappy part of their life
in childhood. Too rigid an upbringing, or rearing that was
chaotic and lacked direction, often causes people to be
neither really in touch with who they are, nor aware of their
real talents.

Do not be surprised if, during the consultation, the
homeopath spends some time leafing through books to
check the signs and symptoms of your disorder, or uses a
computer to analyze your symptom picture. There are over
2,000 remedies used in homeopathic medicine, and it is important to find the one (or ones) most suitable for you.

*Drawing up a disease picture is a complicated process, and modern computer technology can be a great help to the homeopath. When all the essential aspects of the disease picture have been fed in, the computer can produce an analysis, indicating the remedies most likely to be of use, in order of priority. This print-out is an analysis for a middle aged woman suffering from arthritis in the spine and shoulder. The first nine likely remedies are indicated.* Rhus tox *was used to relieve the pain, followed by* Calcarea carbonica *to ease the patient's anxiety state.*

## Working for future health

The homeopath, in considering the build-up of your future health as well as the relief of your current signs and symptoms, will work over a long period to gradually remove some of these different layers of disease. As you become freer and freer, you should begin to approach your perfect health potential. The causes of your ill-health are rooted in these levels of health and various engrafted layers.

When homeopaths talk about susceptibility to disease they are considering all of this. Falling ill with a particular infection or set of signs and symptoms, or development of a chronic condition, is related to your inherited constitution and all the things that have happened to you since you were conceived. These combined experiences make you particularly vulnerable to specific infections, allergic shocks or temporary stresses. This means that when an epidemic arises, and you are under some other prolonged pressure, you – as distinct from anyone else – are predisposed to the development of certain signs and symptoms.

This is reflected in the fact that when an infection spreads among people in an office or a family, some get it and others do not. After an unhappy love affair one person may weather the experience because of strong basic emotional health and self-esteem. Another, who has an inherited weakness and has had some difficulty in childhood, may become quite ill after such a disappointment and exhibit a number of physical, emotional and mental signs and symptoms.

## A case study example

Here is a case study as an example. A man of twenty-eight consulted a homeopath about eczema, which affected his scalp, armpits and pubic areas – that is, all the hairy parts of his body. It was worse late at night and in the early morning, worse for washing with soap, and worse after sweating. The condition was relieved by salt added to his bathwater. In his teens the patient had suffered from asthma and now he tended to become wheezy in cold weather. He recently suffered from thrush of the groin (moniliasis) and in the past had non-specific urethritis. His eyes were sensitive to light and tobacco smoke, which caused swollen eyelids and discharging eyes. He was susceptible to attacks of influenza. The actual signs and symptoms were not particularly serious, although they obviously distressed him.

## SYMPTOM ANALYSIS

| | Rhus toxicodendron | Sulphur | Arsenicum album | Pulsatilla | Calcarea carbonica | Lycopodium | Phosphoricum | Sepia | Ferrum phosphoricum | Nitricum acidum | Nux vomica | Argentum nitricum | Kali carbonicum | Natrum muriaticum |
|---|---|---|---|---|---|---|---|---|---|---|---|---|---|---|
| **Rubrics** | 14 | 11 | 11 | 11 | 12 | 10 | 11 | 11 | 8 | 9 | 10 | 8 | 8 | 9 |
| **Score** | 100 | 78 | 73 | 73 | 67 | 67 | 67 | 65 | 58 | 58 | 54 | 52 | 52 | 52 |
| Extremity Pain; ACHING; Shoulder | 0 | 0 | 0 | 0 | 2 | 0 | 0 | 1 | 0 | 2 | 0 | 0 | 0 | 2 |
| Extremity Pain; ACHING; Knee | 3 | 0 | 0 | 0 | 1 | 1 | 0 | 0 | 0 | 0 | 1 | 0 | 0 | 1 |
| Extremity Pain; ACHING; Hip | 2 | 0 | 0 | 1 | 0 | 0 | 2 | 0 | 0 | 0 | 0 | 0 | 0 | 0 |
| Pain; ACHING; Hip; extending; to ankle | 0 | 0 | 0 | 0 | 0 | 0 | 0 | 0 | 0 | 0 | 0 | 0 | 0 | 0 |
| Extremity Pain; ACHING; Hip; sitting | 2 | 0 | 0 | 0 | 0 | 0 | 0 | 0 | 0 | 0 | 0 | 0 | 0 | 0 |
| Extremity Pain; ACHING; motion amel. | 3 | 0 | 0 | 2 | 0 | 0 | 0 | 0 | 0 | 0 | 0 | 0 | 0 | 0 |
| Extremity Pain; ACHING; waking, on | 0 | 0 | 0 | 1 | 0 | 0 | 0 | 0 | 0 | 0 | 0 | 0 | 0 | 0 |
| Extremity Pain; ACHING; bed, in | 0 | 0 | 0 | 0 | 0 | 0 | 0 | 0 | 0 | 0 | 0 | 0 | 0 | 0 |
| Sleep; POSITION; back, on | 3 | 2 | 1 | 3 | 2 | 2 | 2 | 0 | 2 | 0 | 2 | 0 | 0 | 1 |
| Sleep; UNREFRESHING | 0 | 2 | 2 | 2 | 1 | 2 | 3 | 2 | 0 | 3 | 2 | 2 | 0 | 2 |
| Chest; PAIN; aching; Sides | 1 | 1 | 0 | 0 | 0 | 0 | 0 | 1 | 1 | 0 | 0 | 2 | 0 | 0 |
| PAIN; aching; Dorsal region; scapulae | 1 | 0 | 0 | 0 | 0 | 0 | 1 | 2 | 0 | 0 | 2 | 0 | 0 | 0 |
| Back; PAIN; aching; Dorsal region; spine | 0 | 0 | 0 | 0 | 1 | 0 | 1 | 0 | 0 | 0 | 0 | 0 | 0 | 0 |
| Extremities; COLDNESS; Foot | 2 | 3 | 3 | 3 | 3 | 3 | 3 | 3 | 3 | 3 | 2 | 2 | 3 | 3 |
| Generalities; HEAT; vital, lack of | 3 | 2 | 3 | 0 | 3 | 2 | 3 | 2 | 3 | 3 | 3 | 2 | 3 | 2 |
| Mind; ANXIETY; others, for | 0 | 2 | 2 | 0 | 0 | 0 | 2 | 0 | 0 | 0 | 2 | 2 | 0 | 0 |
| Stomach; DESIRES; bread | 0 | 0 | 2 | 1 | 0 | 0 | 0 | 0 | 2 | 1 | 0 | 0 | 0 | 2 |
| Stomach; DESIRES; sweets | 2 | 3 | 1 | 2 | 2 | 3 | 2 | 2 | 0 | 2 | 1 | 3 | 2 | 1 |
| Mind; STARTING; touched, when | 0 | 0 | 0 | 0 | 0 | 0 | 0 | 0 | 0 | 0 | 0 | 0 | 3 | 0 |
| Mind; STARTING, | 1 | 2 | 3 | 0 | 2 | 2 | 2 | 2 | 0 | 2 | 2 | 0 | 2 | 3 |
| Generalities; MOTION; amel. | 3 | 3 | 2 | 3 | 1 | 3 | 0 | 2 | 3 | 1 | 0 | 2 | 2 | 0 |
| Generalities; MOTION; of affected part amel. | 3 | 3 | 2 | 3 | 1 | 2 | 0 | 2 | 3 | 0 | 0 | 0 | 1 | 0 |
| Generalities; WET; weather | 3 | 2 | 3 | 3 | 3 | 2 | 1 | 2 | 2 | 2 | 2 | 1 | 2 | 0 |

*High or over-achievers who would be lost without the next target and who thrive well under stressful conditions often pay the price of success with an 'irritable' disorder such as eczema.*

However, questioning revealed numerous points about his lifestyle that were aggravating his condition. He worked very long hours, travelling around the world, and frequently moved from one place to another from day to day. In addition to the stress that this put on his relationship with his wife and child, he became very irritable with his colleagues. Even though he suffered from all these problems he had a tremendous restlessness and a desire to travel and to lead a busy life. In fact, during the consultation he had great difficulty sitting still in his chair and often shifted one part or other of his body. His symptoms were worse at night, and better during the day when he was able to move around. However, the story was not all gloom and despondency. Although he was often irritable he did accomplish a great deal and was basically emotionally quite well-balanced. He was ambitious, very active, and gregarious, although ill-health had dented his confidence.

The remedy that he was given was 1M potency of *Rhus toxicodendron* (poison ivy) which, if applied to the skin in a substantial (non-homeopathic) dose, causes very itchy skin eruptions. The particular signs that led to the choice of this remedy rather than another were the tremendous restlessness in the person, restlessness of mind as well as body; the eruptions being mainly on the hairy parts of his body; and his asthmatic breathing in cold weather. Although there were other detailed signs and symptoms that indicated this remedy, these were the outstanding features that led to its prescription.

Within a couple of weeks the eczema had improved a great deal, but the thrush had reappeared. This is an example of signs and symptoms improving in reverse order, and it showed that he was still susceptible to the thrush which had previously been suppressed. No remedy was given for the thrush as such, apart from some bathing in herb teas which relieved it. Soon afterwards, the rest of the physical signs and symptoms disappeared.

The initial remedy continued to be curative, and the man did not return for further consultations until six or seven months later. His skin and his breathing were greatly improved, but the layer to do with his great restlessness and the feeling of 'dis-ease' in his life had worsened. The tension he felt when not travelling or working was increasingly affecting his marriage. This indicated a pattern of behaviour that could be connected with an inherited weakness from tuberculosis, i.e. tuberculosis miasm (see Chapter 3, page 34). So the remedy given was *Tuberculinum* in the 1M potency – that is, using a disease product to clear the level of disease which may have resulted from inherited factors.

### How long is it going to take to get well?

The answer to this question depends on the nature of your diseases, how long you have been ill, the illnesses you have had in the past, your inherited constitution, and the strength of your vital force as a result of all these factors. Sometimes, signs and symptoms that appear trivial or not serious in terms of a threat to your life may have a deep hereditary component in their appearance. For instance, hay fever may persist for two or three years before one can talk about a cure, although each year remedies are given to relieve the acute symptoms, and each year the symptoms may reduce and eventually go away.

On the other hand, a disease normally considered serious and life-threatening, which affects someone having a basically strong constitution with few previous illnesses, may improve rapidly after one or two remedies. Thus it can be seen that the length of time needed for a complete cure may vary greatly. Your homeopath will give you some idea, according to the analysis of your case, of what you might expect and whether you are likely to get any aggravations or old signs and symptoms emerging again as you get better from the inside out.

### The law of cure
The homeopathic ideal is to restore health rapidly, gently and permanently and to remove and destroy the whole disease in the shortest, surest and least harmful way according to clearly understandable principles. However, sometimes the forceful action of the remedy may make certain signs and symptoms stronger temporarily – but this does not mean the disease has got worse. The vital force, in its attempt to restore balance may be throwing more toxic material to the surface as it cleanses the deeper tissues, or throwing out signs and symptoms from the more vital organs to the less vital. For this reason, signs that you have previously had may reappear for a while; or those that you already have, particularly skin conditions, may appear to be worse for some time before they start improving. The law of cure is at work.

It is important to understand that such temporary aggravation of signs and symptoms is often part of the homeopathic process of healing. It is what naturopaths and some other therapists call a healing crisis. If you are not aware of this, you might well feel anxious or upset when signs and symptoms appear after taking a remedy. Do not rush back to using suppressive medicines, such as antibiotics or cortisone creams (except in special circumstances known to your homeopath). This will change the disease picture and hinder the action of the prescribed homeopathic remedy; this in turn will prevent your body's attempt to heal itself from reaching completion.

It is important that you communicate with your homeopath; so if any signs and symptoms arise that you are worried about, don't hesitate: telephone, arrange to see your homeopath at the office, or if really necessary ask for a home visit. Your homeopath is there to help you.

## What if I become ill during treatment?

Some people find that after taking homeopathic remedies for a deep disorder they start having colds and influenza. This may be the system's attempt to detoxify itself in the treatment of a more serious or chronic condition. If the signs and symptoms of the acute illness are not serious, it is very important that no other medication is taken at this point, although natural courses of action such as fasting, drinking fruit juices and taking rest can be useful. If the signs and symptoms drag on, it may be necessary to take a further remedy. Do not treat yourself at this moment, but telephone your homeopath who will then prescribe a remedy that is complementary to the action of the one you have been given for the chronic condition.

It may happen that, after taking a remedy, you simply start feeling better and better without any aggravation. This is a good sign which shows that you probably have a strong constitution and no blocks to the cure. If you do get an acute illness even several weeks or months after your original treatment, you should check with your homeopathic practitioner, because this may be either the emergence of a new pattern or simply the system clearing itself of toxins. If it results from a change in your level of health this is the time when you need to change to another remedy.

After taking a remedy you may feel much better mentally and physically, and more able to face the world. You may suddenly decide to make that change in your career that you have been thinking about for some time; your relationship with your partner may begin to improve; perhaps a seemingly impossible problem will finally be resolved as a result of standing up for yourself and refusing to take any more of the behaviour that was upsetting you so much. You may find that because you are becoming more at ease with other people, you start making new friends or exploring new ventures. Even though you may still have some of the signs and symptoms that prompted you to seek the help of a homeopath, the fact that these changes are taking place shows that the remedy has started to heal the whole person.

Sometimes the first observation patients report after taking a remedy is a feeling of extreme well-being, of peace within themselves and an increase in energy – sometimes so much energy that they do not know what to do with it. At other times, people report that they simply feel better in themselves in some way that is difficult to describe. All these reactions are indications that the remedy is working. If you do have a serious condition the improvement may be slow and the signs small, but there will be something to show your progress. One patient who was still depressed and having many problems to work out in her life, said at the end of a consultation: 'Well, I may still be wanting to die but I'm no longer wanting to kill myself.' That was a month after the initial consultation.

It is useful for you as well as your homeopath to keep a record of the changes that go on during the time between consultations after taking each remedy, so that you can see whether it is acting or whether some other treatment is required.

### How can I help myself?

In general, homeopathic practitioners accept the way in which their patients choose to live and do not lay down any strict rules about diet, unless the condition is serious enough to demand it. Neither do they require that you drastically change your lifestyle if you want homeopathic treatment. But there are some alterations that you may need to make in order to allow the remedies to work well for you.

The change that you are most likely to be asked to make is to stop drinking coffee, at least until your health is substantially improved. This is not only because coffee is quite a strong drug in itself, with a whole symptom picture of its own, but also because with experience homeopaths have found that caffeine from coffee is easily assimilated into the bloodstream. Coffee can have an adverse effect on the action of the remedy, which therefore means that your signs and symptoms are more likely to relapse; so the remedy will need repeating more frequently for any progress to be made at all. However, it takes a lot to counteract the effect of a remedy that really suits an individual. If certain remedies are prescribed, the homeopath may also ask you to cut out the use of menthol, eucalyptus, camphor and other strongly aromatic oils. This may mean changing to a more mildly flavoured toothpaste, giving up eating strong mints and chewing minty gum, and avoiding the use of vapour rubs and inhalants.

If your condition seems to indicate the need, your homeopath may make recommendations about your diet and suggest some exercises, as well as prescribing a remedy. A reduction in your consumption of alcohol could be

*Coffee is a stimulant drug and can affect your behaviour and any disease picture you may present at a homeopathic consultation. You should avoid coffee altogether during homeopathic treatment, as it inhibits the action of the remedies.*

requested, but there will be no coercion to make you give it up altogether, unless you are seriously ill.

The oral contraceptive pill can adversely affect a woman's total health, because it continually changes her balance of hormones. Some homeopathic practitioners will not treat women who are taking it. However, it should become obvious during treatment that only a certain level of improvement is possible while the pill is being taken. As they become more aware of their health and self-healing processes, many women decide during treatment to start using a different method of contraception.

If, when you go for a consultation, you are already taking medication prescribed from a previous treatment for a condition such as asthma, a heart disorder, anxiety or depression, tell your practitioner about it. You may need to continue taking the previous medication as well as the homeopathic remedies for some time.

As you improve with homeopathy, your medication will slowly be reduced and in many cases eventually stopped altogether. The length of time this takes depends on how long you have had your condition.

*Homeopathy is a safe therapy for young people and children as it is very specific. It does not flood their systems with the unwanted side-effects of broad spectrum drugs, but rather strengthens their constitutions so that they become robust enough to throw off most bacterial or viral intrusions.*

If an endocrine gland, such as the thyroid which secretes the hormone thyroxine, has been removed or has atrophied, then obviously you will be dependent on a replacement of the appropriate hormone. But if the gland is not completely atrophied, it may be possible to stimulate what is left of it to produce more of its hormone and so enable you to come slowly off the supplement, or at least to reduce it.

Some diabetics who have had their condition for a long time – especially since childhood – may have to remain completely dependent on insulin, but even so it may be possible to reduce the daily amount needed.

When children are treated for chronic conditions and other disorders, their response to homeopathic treatment is often much faster than that of adults. At this stage in their development, young people have had fewer setbacks in their lives (emotional or physical), to stand in the way of their improvement. Most normal, growing children have plenty of vitality; therefore they tend to recover from illness more quickly than adults.

*Homeopathy is equally suitable for older people, who may often be made to feel more ill by the side-effects of powerful drugs than the original reason for the medication. A strong constitution, which homeopathy fosters as much as possible, will also allow them to enjoy an active old age.*

Where extensive tissue changes have been brought about by long-standing chronic conditions, particularly in elderly people, it may not be possible to effect a complete cure. Nonetheless, it should be possible to relieve suffering, gain some improvement in signs and symptoms, and create a greater sense of well-being. The more actively a patient is willing to participate and co-operate with the homeopath and take responsibility for maintaining health in other areas of life, the more quickly he or she is likely to get well again.

### The best sources of remedies

It is important that remedies are bought from manufacturing pharmacies of good reputation. Some pharmacies do not prepare the remedies properly, either giving an inadequate amount of succussion or by using machines that perform the succussion in a different way, for example by using ultra-sound or by shooting a jet of water into a vat. Such remedies may be all right, but they should not be used unless they have been re-proved to check that they produce the same results. Classical homeopathic practitioners endeavour to support and recommend those pharmacies which they believe to be conscientious in following the rules of homeopathic pharmacy. The best pharmacies are served by people dedicated to homeopathic ideals.

Many practitioners, not knowing exactly which pharmacy is producing the most effective remedies, give a patient several doses of the same remedy made by different pharmacies, to be taken within a few hours of each other, to make sure that the remedy acts. Otherwise if there is no improvement in the patient's condition, it is difficult for the practitioner to assess whether the remedy was not properly potentized, or whether there was some other obstacle to cure.

There is not much money to be made from homeopathic pharmaceuticals, as there is from the expensive chemicals produced by the allopathic drug companies of the world. It does not take many pharmacies to supply the homeopathic needs of the whole world. For this reason, it is easy to understand why the international drug companies, which stand to profit so much from their businesses, are often so antagonistic to homeopathic medicine. If there continued to be the same rate of growth as there is now in the numbers of people turning to homeopathic treatment worldwide, it would put many major drug companies out of business, and greatly reduce the profitability of those remaining.

Laboratories used by homeopathic pharmacies must be kept spotlessly clean in order to ensure that the remedies are not contaminated in any way during manufacture. Mother tinctures must be very carefully preserved in glass bottles for future use. The tops of phials of potentized remedies need to be stoppered with cork or with screw-top lids lined with cork. Some pharmacies now use plastic containers to package their wares for the shops, instead of the more inert glass. Some homeopaths believe that the petrochemical fumes, however minimal, given off by plastics have a neutralizing effect on the remedies. I certainly always purchase glass-stored remedies myself.

If a powder or tablet is to be stored temporarily before administration in prescribed doses, it is often wrapped in a clean, unused piece of good quality paper; this is adequate for such temporary storage, which is generally only for a few days at most.

People travelling abroad with homeopathic remedies these days should keep the bottles in their hand luggage, and insist that customs officers should examine such bags physically rather than putting them through the X-ray scanners which are used for much hand luggage. The X-rays can have a deleterious effect on the remedies.

*A homeopathic pharmacy, where prescribed homeopathic remedies can be made up. It is possible to buy remedies over the counter in other shops, but it is always better to consult a homeopath. Each diagnosis is unique and specific: the remedy that suits one person will not match another's particular symptoms: and what is effective at one time in your life may not work at another.*

## CASE HISTORIES

### GLANDULAR FEVER

A woman aged 23 was suffering from infectious *mononucleosis,* or glandular fever. She was a pale, slight woman with sandy-coloured hair; she had a job and was also studying. She was conscientious, but lacked confidence.

Her symptoms were swollen glands at the back of her neck and in the armpits, with burning pains in her wrists, fingers, ankles, and right hip. Her throat ached, her chest felt infected, and her breasts were tender. She had a feeling of pressure over the eyes, which was worse when she was studying, and her concentration was poor. She needed a lot of sleep and had difficulty waking up. She felt chilly, but had a raised temperature; although she preferred cold food to hot.

She was prescribed *Silica* 10M. At first her joints became more swollen, then less so. Her glands stopped hurting, her energy increased and she was able to get up more easily. A month later she reported that she had no headaches and her concentration was improving, and she was not too worried about her exams. Her last period was not painful, though her breasts and armpits were tender at that time.

Two months later she had developed a catarrhal sinusitis, found breathing difficult in the mornings, and was coughing up thick mucus. Her sinuses improved with rubbing and fresh air. She disclosed that she had a history of swollen adenoids. *Pulsatilla* 6x three times a day was prescribed.

Seven months later she reported that she felt tired in the afternoons, and had a blocked nose alternating with a watery discharge. Her glands and tonsils swelled occasionally and she had been getting fevers and night sweats. She had passed her exams and had more responsibility in her job. She was again given *Silica* 10M, and improved as a result.

### GASTROENTERITIS

The patient was a baby boy, nine months old, suffering from gastroenteritis, with diarrhoea and vomiting, caused by a bacterial infection. It was summer time, and the boy was teething. His mother telephoned from hospital to say that the baby had not been able to keep down any food or drink for a few days. He was rapidly dehydrating because, although he was on a saline and glucose drip, his veins kept closing on the drip; he was showing signs of starvation. The diarrhoea was watery, mucousy, profuse and apparently painless. He was weak and not able to sit up; his face was pale, though he flushed occasionally; his eyes were sunken and had blue marks around them. His abdomen was distended and he gagged and vomited when given any liquid by mouth.

The prescription was *Podophyllum* 30c, a remedy prepared from the root of the North American herb may-apple. Several tablets of the medicine were crushed in sterile water. The baby's lips were wetted with the liquid, at first every ten minutes, as he improved half-hourly, and then hourly. He responded and within a day he was off the drip. After the first day the *Podophyllum* was reduced to one dose every few hours. Several days later he was strong enough to leave hospital and was breast-feeding again.

Because the child was weakened by this episode his general development was set back. So he was given *Phosphoricum acidum* 200c (phosphoric acid) for weakness following loss of fluids, and then *Calcarea carbonica* 200c for sweatiness, lack of good muscle tone, and ailments while teething. Two months later the boy's development was back to average.

## DEPRESSION

A 26-year-old woman sought treatment for a flare-up of cracked, itchy, allergic eczema on her feet. *Graphites* was prescribed, but there was not much change in her condition.

Two weeks later the patient telephoned on a Sunday. This time she revealed that she had been raped the year before. The trial of the man accused was due shortly and she was going to have to give evidence. She dreaded reliving the episode in court. Her skin was worse, she was very depressed, and wanted to sleep all day or be alone, listening to music. At night she was sleepless and frightened.

She felt light-headed and dizzy, as if she were drunk, and in this state had walked into a lamp-post. She was in a suicidal state: she had a strong desire to take an overdose of some tranquillizers which her general practitioner had prescribed for her. She avoided doing that by asking a friend to stay with her. She was constantly weeping and had a strong feeling of self-condemnation. She felt weak and her head ached.

*Aurum metallicum* 6c was given in repeated doses; because it was Sunday it was not possible to obtain a higher potency. Two days later *Aurum met* 30c was administered. Within a few days the woman had come out of her acute depression. Although there are several remedies suitable for suicidal feelings, *Aurum,* a remedy prepared from metallic gold, was chosen because of the additional symptoms of dizziness in the open air, the sense of self-condemnation, and the desire to listen to music after a shock. In a couple of weeks her skin was improving, too; this was interesting because *Aurum* is not normally indicated for eczema or other skin troubles.

## HEPATITIS

A 28-year-old woman had been suffering from hepatitis (inflammation of the liver) for a month. So far she had treated it first by fasting and then by adopting a very plain diet. She was thirsty, lacking in energy, and wanting to sleep a lot.

There was an ache in the liver area which was worse when she was tired. She had a slight nausea which was relieved by eating. She fancied sweet things in spite of her condition. If her bowels were upset she lost her appetite; her motions had been loose and pale. Generally she had a feeling of anxiety which upset her bowels, and she had a history of weakness in the digestive system. She tended to be pale and to catch colds and influenza readily. She showed a strong tendency to hypochondria. There was no history of childhood diseases.

Her self-confidence was low; she had anxious dreams, and was often worried before parties; she had to make herself go to such gatherings, but always enjoyed herself when there. Although she liked people she had difficulty in forming close relationships; she had sought psychotherapeutic help for this problem.

The woman was prescribed *Lycopodium* 6 three times a day for a week. This brought an improvement. *Lycopodium,* a preparation of club-moss, was chosen – as opposed to other remedies such as *Chelidonium* (celandine) which are good for the liver and particularly for hepatitis – because of the need for her to eat frequently and her strong desire for sweets. In addition to the digestive symptoms, her anxious personality and lack of self-confidence, although she was gregarious, pointed to *Lycopodium.* After one week there was an improvement, but she was still tired. She was then prescribed three doses of *Lycopodium* 30c, and the improvement continued.

## SCIATICA

A young woman suffering from chronic psoriasis (a common relapsing scaly skin disease) and arthritis developed acute sciatica. The pain extended from the lumbar region of the back, through the right buttock, across the hips, and down the legs. She was stiff when rising from a chair, and sudden movement produced a sharp pain; gentle movement ameliorated the pain. She was comfortable only when lying on her back, but changing position in bed was very uncomfortable. There was occasional pain in the left shoulder blade. Massage and heat provided some relief.

The woman felt irritable and impatient. For the past six months she had had chronic, watery diarrhoea, preceded by cramps in the abdomen.

The prescription was *Gnaphthalium* 1M. This remedy was indicated for the patient's sciatic symptoms and also for the arthritis and the diarrhoea. Improvement of the sciatic pains began within 12 hours, and continued for three weeks. Then she relapsed, with the pain centred in her hips and thighs, alternately in the right and left legs.

*Gnaphthalium* 1M was repeated. A further acute condition arose after this as a healing crisis. She had aching joints and influenza-like symptoms; the arthritis in the left knee was much worse, and her bones ached as if they were going to break. She was nauseated and vomiting, thirsty for water. There was pain all over the head, and her tongue was coated. She was weak, pale, sleeping a lot, and cold and shivery at night. For this she was prescribed *Eupatorium perfoliatum* 30c. She improved after that.

## CASE HISTORIES

### THE DISRUPTIVE CHILD

This was a case of very restless, violent behaviour in a child aged two years and ten months. He had previously had homeopathic treatment for a tendency to sudden fevers, threadworms and whitlows. He had been given *Belladonna, Cina* (worm-seed), *Teucrium marum* (cat-thyme), and *Silica.*

He had developed aggressive behaviour, loved fighting and wrestling, even with much bigger boys, and seemed fearless. He behaved worst when he was on his own, and sought the company of his friends all the time, but he was being rejected by other children in his neighbourhood because of his conduct.

At home he was disobedient and obstinate, though he would also repent and be very loving. He refused to use the toilet, though he knew how to. He threw water around the bathroom, leaped all over the furniture, was jealous of his brother, and demanded attention.

He was afraid of swimming and hated having his hair washed. He said his abdomen hurt when he was sitting down. He had recently developed a fear of dogs, was afraid of the dark and had difficulty in going to sleep.

Because his mother had had tuberculosis as a child, the boy was initially given a dose of the nosode *Tuberculinum,* which is indicated for restlessness, irritability, fear of dogs, and tendency to swollen glands. Although this produced a slight improvement it did not last.

It became clearer that his fear of the dark, his inability to go to sleep, his mental excitement and continued and growing violence – despite his frequent repentance – were the dominant factors. So he was given *Stramonium* 30c (a preparation of thorn-apple). This remedy is indicated for these strong mental and behavioural symptoms. It also related to his history of fevers which had responded well to *Belladonna,* a related remedy of the same botanical family, Solanaceae.

Within a couple of weeks there was a great improvement: he had become much less violent and restless, more gentle and friendly, and was starting to use the toilet properly.

## VARICOSE VEINS

The patient, a man of 63, had varicose veins in his left calf. The veins protruded from the leg but they were painless. His ankle was swollen and discoloured in the evenings. He had had a tendency to varicose veins and swelling over the previous ten years, but the condition, which now included psoriasis (a scaly skin complaint) of the left foot, had recently deteriorated. He was heavily built, although not overweight, and in recent years he had started to become clumsy. He felt the cold. Although susceptible to diarrhoea in summer, he had a history of constipation as a child.

After the patient's tonsils and adenoids were removed in childhood, hay fever developed. This condition, for which he took Beconaze, now occurred annually. His eyes itched and the whites of his eyes were chronically red. On waking, his mouth was dry and he had catarrh in the throat. When he was 25 he had had an operation for an umbilical hernia.

He had suffered from high blood pressure in the past, while he was worried about his wife who was ill; his condition had improved with exercise, diet, and biofeedback which helped him to relax. Otherwise he had been healthy and energetic.

He still had an aversion to salt, which he had given up because of the blood pressure problem. Pasta, Italian food and fish appealed to him, but he had a strong dislike of onions and garlic. He was thirsty for coffee and fruit juice.

This patient enjoyed work and found it hard to relax; however, he would worry if he did not try to do so. He was less gregarious than his wife, but they had a happy marriage. He was now able to talk about his feelings and cry when he was sad. His memory for people was not so good as it had been.

The painless varicose veins on the leg, the previous enlarged tonsils and the umbilical hernia, combined with the coldness, susceptibility to diarrhoea for which he felt worse, a degree of anxiety and his heavy build, led to a prescription of *Calcarea carbonica* 200c.

After a month his left ankle was less swollen and the psoriasis on his foot was smaller. He felt better for the warm weather, and his hay fever was improved. His bowels were normal.

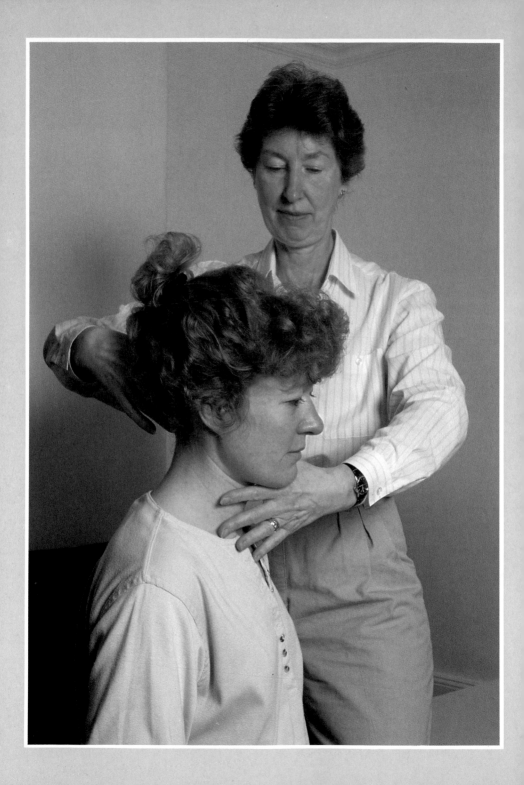

# 6

# RELATED THERAPIES

A t this point you may be asking: 'Will homeopathy be enough to make me better?' In many cases the answer is 'Yes'. But there are some conditions where there is an obstacle to cure which is nutritional, or mechanical – such as a misaligned joint for example. In these cases, a therapy complementary or supplementary to homeopathy may be needed. A number of other therapies may be considered as complementary, and some are described here. They are listed in alphabetical order for ease of reference, but they can also be grouped by type.

The first group includes therapies aimed at manipulating the muscles and joints of the body to relieve pain and promote general health. They are osteopathy and chiropractic, both of which concentrate largely on the spine; the Alexander technique, which is largely concerned with posture; reflexology, which regards the feet as the key to ailments in the rest of the body; hydrotherapy and massage, which are techniques employed in several of the other therapies. Herbalism and naturopathy are therapies that rely on natural substances and dieting, and seek to correct unhealthy ways of life. Yoga, acupuncture and ayurvedic medicine are oriental therapies which are coming into increasing use in the West.

All the treatments begin with a careful study of the patient, and the taking of a case-history. In addition some systems of treatment have their own methods of diagnosis. They include iris diagnosis, Ayurvedic and Chinese pulse-taking, observing different signs on the tongue, and analysis of such substances as hair and sweat.

Therapies that work on the mind and are of particular value in treating emotional upsets include psychotherapy, hypnotherapy, and counselling of various kinds.

Healing belongs in none of these categories, but undoubtedly has a beneficial effect on the mind, emotions and subtle energies, and through them, on the physical body. Anthroposophy is an offshoot of homeopathy, but is as much a way of life as a medical therapy.

### What is acupuncture?

Acupuncture is one of the oldest systems of medicine in the world. It has been practised in China for at least 5,000 years, and is used in Japan and most countries of eastern and southeastern Asia. Acupuncture was unknown in the West until about 350 years ago, and did not become really well known

*It is obvious that every reasonable physician will first of all remove the exciting or sustaining cause (causa occasionalis). After that the indisposition usually disappears on its own.*

Samuel Hahnemann

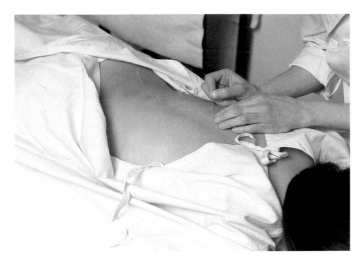

*Acupuncture shares with homeopathy the idea of the body as self healing, given the right help. In acupuncture, help is given by stimulating or regulating with needles the flow of* Chi, *or life force, via acupuncture points along the paths of the meridians which network the body.*

here until the 1950s. Acupuncture specialists now practise in Britain, France, West Germany, the Soviet Union and the United States.

Acupuncture therapy consists of inserting very fine needles into special parts of the body, called acupuncture points. Chinese practitioners believe that this treatment relieves pain, treats disease, and restores the balance of *chi* energy – equivalent to the vital force described by Hahnemann. There are 365 points on the body at which the needles may be inserted. The patient feels a slight prick as the needles pierce the skin, but usually suffers no further discomfort.

The acupuncturist may leave some needles stationary, rotate others, or move them in and out. In a modern variant of acupuncture, a low-voltage electric current is passed through the needles. The period of treatment varies, and may last up to an hour.

Acupuncture is used for treating a great variety of ailments, particularly complaints such as headaches and arthritis. In recent years it has been used in China instead of anaesthesia, even in major surgery, and for the relief of post–operative pain.

Although there is, at first glance, no obvious reason why acupuncture should work, it does. Recent medical research into acupuncture has come up with the theory that the needles may help the body to secrete enkephalins – natural substances found in the nervous system and other parts of

the body. The role of enkephalins is not yet fully understood, but it is believed that they have a morphine-like effect
and are involved in the transmission or suppression of pain.
However, practitioners of traditional Chinese medicine
oppose the reduction of this comprehensive health care
system to a method of pain control because they believe it
has a much wider scope.

### Can acupuncture complement homeopathy?

Although acupuncture is a parallel system to homeopathy in
that they both act on the vital force, the two therapies do not
easily complement each other. The action of one may
actually interfere with the action and healing powers of the
other. For this reason, if patients want to use acupuncture,
homeopaths generally suggest to them that they go and take
a course of it, and then come back if they want to return to
homeopathic treatment. There are times when, it seems,
acupuncture will do things that homeopathy cannot, and
vice versa. So there are occasions for using either of the
therapies but as a general rule they should not be used at the
same time.

### The Alexander technique

One of several therapies aimed at correcting some structural
malposition in the body, the Alexander technique was
devised about the turn of the century by an Australian actor,
F. Matthias Alexander (1869-1955), to overcome a personal
problem: he kept losing his voice during performances, and
this was threatening his career. Realizing that he must be
doing something wrong, he tried reciting in front of a
mirror. He noticed that he had many bodily tensions and
bad postural habits, and discovered that these were the cause
of his periodic loss of voice.

Alexander also observed that young children, from soon
after birth to about the age of two, moved easily and
naturally, and were relaxed in their movements. As they
grew older and copied the postural example of their elders,
they lost this fluid dynamic balance. Young children, in
their desire to learn, often copy adult patterns of behaviour
that are not necessarily conducive to good health.

Alexander devised a system of treatment that is very hard
to describe on paper – it has to be demonstrated, because it
varies for each person according to need. An Alexander
teacher helps the patient to get rid of bad habits of posture

which are damaging health by creating muscular and skeletal tensions. Bad posture can lead to a number of problems, such as lower back pain and headaches. By correcting postural defects, these troubles often disappear. Homeopaths realize this, and may suggest a course of sessions instead of medicines. A number of prominent people have found the Alexander technique beneficial, among them the American philosopher and educator John Dewey and the British novelist Aldous Huxley.

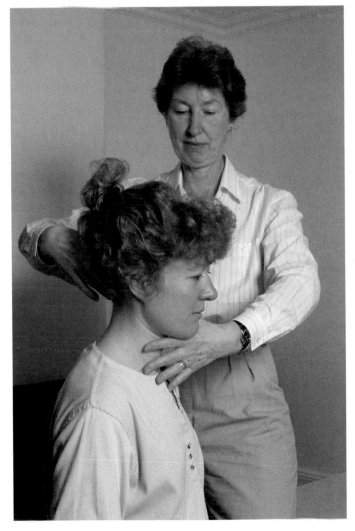

*The Alexander technique re-trains the body gently to correct posture, encouraging the dumping of years of bad habits and unnecessary effort. It teaches the most efficient and relaxed way to use your body to the full and is an excellent method of dealing with stress.*

### Anthroposophical medicine

The spiritual and mystical doctrine called anthroposophy was founded in 1909 by the Austrian social philosopher Rudolf Steiner (1861–1925). He coined the name from two Greek words meaning 'man' and 'divine wisdom'. Anthroposophy includes its own system of medicine, which is an offshoot of homeopathy but differs from it in many ways.

As a young man Steiner edited the scientific writings of the German poet, scientist and statesman Johann von Goethe, and was greatly influenced by Goethe's ideas. Goethe himself was a contemporary of Hahnemann, and appears to have been affected by Hahnemann's work.

Steiner did not fully grasp the teachings of Hahnemann, however, and mixed them with his own ideas. His medicines were diluted but not always succussed, the process Hahnemann always considered the best for making homeopathic remedies. Today anthroposophical remedies are often potentized by centrifuge, or not potentized at all but merely diluted. In anthroposophical medicine, remedies are prescribed on their affinity to a certain organ of the body, and some were chosen from the so-called 'Doctrine of Signatures' (see Chapter 7) – some character of a plant such as colour, shape or habitat indicating its supposed affinity with part of the body. In this way Steiner used some materials that were not in the homeopathic pharmacy, and without 'proving' his remedies homeopathically.

Remedies in different potencies are often mixed together because some of the symptom pictures of each cover similar symptoms in particular diseases. These multiple remedies have names such as *Dermatodron*, for skin conditions; *Digestoron*, for the stomach; *Pneumodoron*, for lung disorders; *Hepatodoron* for the liver; and *Menodoron*, for menstrual disorders. Anthroposophical practitioners often inject remedies into the affected area of the body. In other words, anthroposophical medicine uses some potentized remedies as does homeopathy, but in a very different way from that taught by Hahnemann.

Steiner divided his model into three systems:

- *Nerves and senses, providing also the functions of sense perception and thinking*
- *Metabolism and musculo-skeletal system, from which the function of will is manifested*
- *Circulation and respiration, connected with feeling.*

Steiner classified illnesses according to their affinity to a particular system. He regarded the three systems as interconnected, and also acting with an interpenetrating etheric body. This, he believed, creates the life pattern and takes up the same space as the physical body, becoming separated from it at death. In addition Steiner postulated the existence of an astral body, which is to do with a person's emotions and desires; and an ego body, which is connected with consciousness of self.

> '*Ego Body is spirit, associated with heat and fire; Astral Body is feeling, associated with air; Etheric Body is associated with the element water; and Physical Body is associated with the Earth.*'

These four bodies correspond to the medieval idea of the humours and elements. There is also a connection here with Chinese and Ayurvedic medicine, the ideas of which were probably introduced into Europe from Asia by traders, or by the armies of Alexander the Great returning from India.

Anthroposophical medicine is practised by qualified doctors who have also studied anthroposophy. It is more popular in continental Europe than in Britain, where it was introduced by practitioners fleeing from the Nazis in the 1930s. There is a postgraduate training centre for physicians in Switzerland.

## Ayurvedic medicine

Homeopathy is also much used by the practitioners of Ayurvedic medicine, the classical medical tradition of India, which incorporates many healing methods. As far as homeopathy is concerned, its proponents claim that Hahnemann himself owed much of his theory of homeopathy to Ayurvedic theories. Ayurvedic medicine has used homeopathy since it was introduced into India by the British at the end of the nineteenth century.

## What is Ayurvedic medicine?

The name Ayurveda comes from the Sanskrit, and means 'knowledge of long life'. It has been practised for at least 2,600 years, and the oldest book of Ayurvedic medicine was compiled in the sixth century BC. The system is not viewed just as a way of curing disease, but as a positive way of prolonging a healthy life.

Traditional Ayurvedic texts regard the body as being made up of five elements: earth, water, fire, wind, and space. Each element has its own corresponding physical sense and is represented in the body by an organ, a bodily fluid or a function.

*According to Ayurvedic medicine, the elements that rage outside our bodies – earth, wind, water, fire and space – are reflected within the human body. Here they combine to form the three doshas, or energy sources which, when they work in harmony, promote good health.*

- *Earth has the quality of smell; it is the most solid, and is represented in the body by the solid organs.*
- *Water has the quality of taste, and is represented in the body by phlegm.*
- *Fire's qualities are beauty and light; it is represented in the body by bile, which is thought of as digesting the food.*
- *Wind has the quality of touch, and is represented in the body by breath, speech, excretion and childbirth.*
- *Space has the quality of sound; it is represented in the body by the hollow organs such as the stomach.*

The ancient writers say that the five elements combine to form three *doshas*, or sources of energy in the body. Wind and space combine to form *vata*, the energy behind movement, earth and water combine as *kapha*, the energy of cohesion, and fire blazes alone as *pitta* the energy that transforms. The correct balance of the *doshas* is considered essential for the preservation or restoration of good health.

**Ayurvedic medicine today**
Today, Ayurvedic medicine flourishes in India, where there are at least 500,000 Ayurvedic practitioners. Under government auspices Ayurvedic physicians undergo a rigorous seven-and-a-half year university training in Ayurvedic surgery and medicine, followed by a course in which they study Western medicine and its relation to their own system. Ayurvedic doctors make use of modern Western medical techniques, such as X-rays and blood tests, and work alongside doctors trained in Western medicine. In addition, they use a great variety of traditional therapies to restore the *doshas* to their correct balance, including acupuncture, herbalism, homeopathy, hydrotherapy, massage, osteopathy, and yoga.

Ayurvedic medicine spread to Arabia, China, Japan, Persia (Iran) and Tibet in ancient times, and has in turn absorbed medical theories from these cultures. It was formally established in Britain in 1982, when the Association of Ayurvedic Practitioners was formed.

### Chiropractic

*Chiropractic is based on the idea that positive health is dependent on the correct position and function of the spine. The art of chiropractic consists in the successful manipulation of the spine to restore it to its optimum performance level.*

Chiropractic is a system for treating mechanical disorders of the joints, especially those of the spine. The principles of chiropractic were laid down in 1895 by a Canadian-born healer, David Daniel Palmer.

Although D. D. Palmer was not actually medically qualified, he had made a study of both anatomy and physiology. From what he read he concluded that misplacement of the vertebrae could be responsible for disease because of its effect on the nervous system. Palmer's ideas are similar in principle to those of osteopathy, founded 21 years earlier by Dr Andrew Taylor Still. Indeed, Palmer was once a student

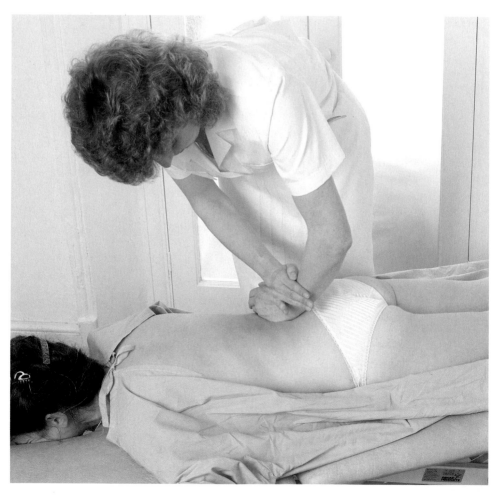

of Still. A major element of chiropractic therapy is centred on the spine and its manipulation and adjustment to bring about a cure.

Chiropractors use orthodox techniques of taking case histories and diagnoses. They make use of X-rays to help in diagnosis, and to check on progress during treatment. They use their hands to detect changes in the spine, and manipulation to correct those changes. Chiropractors claim their work is particularly useful in treating pain in the back and neck, sciatica, and some muscular aches. They also report success in dealing with the complaint known as 'frozen shoulder', often suffered by people playing sport or doing work that requires a lot of shoulder strain, such as house painting or playing the violin. While homeopathy can effectively treat pain in both bones and muscles, it cannot deal with misaligned joints. Your homeopathic practitioner may therefore recommend a visit to a chiropractor to eliminate the root cause of such problems.

Chiropractic is particularly popular in the United States, where there are several chiropractic colleges offering a four-year degree course, and all chiropractors must pass an examination to obtain a licence to practice.

## Healing

Many other techniques can be used to supplement homeopathic therapy. One that is particularly beneficial to some people is healing – the modern term for faith healing, spiritual healing or energetic healing. All the world's great religions have some sort of spiritual healing as part of their tradition, and indeed for many centuries, priests and other religious people often provided the main medical services.

There are many trained healers who have had careful preparation for using the healing energy they possess. This healing energy cannot be learned, but some people are born with the ability to recognize and use it. It is not necessary for people to believe in religion or the healing force to benefit from it, but of course any therapy which works on a patient's mind also affects the emotions and thereby the physical state.

The powers of healers are so far little understood, even by healers themselves. Some researchers think that the healers can somehow, by laying on of hands, prayer or other methods, transfer some of their own inner energy to their patients.

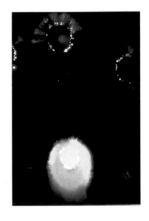

*A remarkable Kirlian photograph of the hands of a healer at work. Kirlian photographs measure the high energy interchange between the subject and an applied electrical field. There is controversy whether or not this photograph goes any way to prove the existence of healing powers.*

### Herbalism

Many people confuse homeopathy with herbalism, simply because some homeopathic remedies are made from herbs and other plants; but then, so are many allopathic medicines, such as digitalis (the heart medicine derived from foxglove). There is a world of difference between homeopathy and herbalism. For one thing, homeopathic medicines are taken in very dilute form, whereas herbal infusions are often taken in large amounts. Although some of the herbs used by herbalists are also used to prepare homeopathic medicines, many are not. Many herbalists are allopathic in their approach, tending to regard the symptoms of the disease as their primary target, and do not build up the same 'disease picture' as homeopathic practitioners.

Occasionally a homeopath prescribes a herbal remedy to a patient. If so the remedy is one which – if given in a very large dose – would produce similar signs and symptoms to those of the patient. The remedy is generally in the form of a mother tincture – that is, the basic extract of the herb from which the higher potencies are made – and of course in small doses.

However, it should be stated that the school of herbalism that developed in The United States in the nineteenth century was very much affected by the work of the homeopaths practising there at that time. Many of the remedies prescribed by present-day American herbalists are to some degree homeopathic in their curative action.

Herbal medicine is also one of the four branches of Chinese medicine (the others are acupuncture, diet and massage). Chinese methods of diagnosis are more carefully thought-out than a great deal of Western herbalism, and have a tradition and literature going back thousands of years.

Western herbalism dates back to the days of Ancient Egypt, and possibly beyond. Its principles were formed from the collected experience of many people, often country folk who had intimate knowledge of their plants and also understood the best times to gather them. For many hundreds of years herbalism was allied to astrology and magic, even in the writings of such a distinguished physician as the seventeenth-century English doctor Nicholas Culpeper. This ultimately gave herbalism a bad name. Modern well-trained herbalists do in fact have a great deal of therapeutic knowledge. So, although homeopathy and her-

*An Arabic herbal from 1334. Herbalism is an ancient medical therapy which has been practised all over the world (with variations depending on the local flora) since primitive times.*

balism have areas of similarity, their basic principles are very different. Most homeopaths would not recommend a patient to take homeopathic and herbal remedies at the same time.

## Hydrotherapy

The ancient art of hydrotherapy employs water for treating people. It can be used on its own or in addition to other forms of treatment, such as naturopathy, homeopathy and physiotherapy. It has been practised since the days of ancient Greece and Rome, when natural sources of water were the first to be used. There are many springs where the

*The French spa town of Vichy first acquired fame for its alkaline springs in the 17th century.*

water is rich in minerals; such water is generally taken internally. Others originate near underground sources of heat, and come to the surface at high temperatures. These sources of water are known as spas after the Belgian town of Spa, a health resort to which people have flocked since the 1500s. A homeopath may recommend hydrotherapy for its refreshing, revitalizing properties during convalescence, for instance.

Water at any temperature can be used for therapeutic purposes, and some simple treatments may easily be followed at home. The physiotherapy departments of many hospitals have heated hydrotherapy pools where patients can be treated. Because water supports the body, patients with disabilities are able to exercise with minimum effort for themselves and the physiotherapists. Such treatment is of particular value for people with handicaps such as spastics, or those recovering the use of limbs following a stroke. Physicians often prescribe alternate treatments with hot and cold water to stimulate the circulation of the blood. European hydrotherapists use cold water baths and sprays to treat obesity and respiratory ailments, and claim to have a high success rate.

## Hypnotherapy

Homeopaths sometimes use hypnotherapy as an adjunct to homeopathic treatment in cases of addiciton or obsessive anxiety. The therapeutic use of hypnosis is said to have been founded by the Austrian physician Franz Anton Mesmer (1734–1815), who gave his name to mesmerism, the practice of imposing a hypnotic state upon a subject. Mesmer enjoyed a large and aristocratic practice in Paris, where his patients included the queen, Marie Antoinette. But many of his fellow doctors considered him a fraud and, after the French Revolution began, he fled to Switzerland, ruined and discredited.

Modern hypnotherapists describe hypnosis as one of the tools used in the process of psychoanalysis, and indeed Sigmund Freud, the founder of psychoanalysis, used hypnotherapy in his early days.

Present-day hypnotherapists include many medically-qualified people. Patients consulting a hypnotherapist are taken into a state of complete relaxation – a 'trance'. While they are in that state the hypnotherapist can help them to change negative mental patterns which may be causing their

*Hypnotherapy, which puts the patient directly in touch with his unconscious, can be a useful adjunct to any health therapy. It is particularly beneficial as an anaesthetic, and as an aid to curing addiction.*

illness, and replace them with positive ones. When hypnotherapy is used to treat psychiatric illnesses, such as phobias, it probably needs to be reinforced with other treatment, and here homeopathy can help by prescribing remedies that reflect a patient's mental symptoms. Contrary to popular belief, there is no fear that a hypnotised person may be made to commit a crime or any other act that is against his or her normal inclination.

## Iridology

Iris diagnosis (also known as iridology), is a diagnostic method that developed during the last century. By observing markings in the iris of the eye, any areas of the body which may be disordered, poisoned, or degenerated may be identified. It is well-known that the condition of the eyes can often give clues to the physical state of patients, and doctors commonly look at them in the course of a routine examination. Specialists in iridology believe that the unique colour and structure of the iris can tell them much more than is generally realized, giving advance warning of an impending disease state before the patient experiences any pathological symptoms.

Iridologists illuminate the patient's eyes with a pen light and examine the iris with a magnifying glass. A modern procedure is to use special photographic techniques to produce colour slides of the eyes, which can then be enlarged by projecting them on to a screen for detailed examination. The iridologist can study the slides at leisure and form the diagnosis; at a second visit the patient is told what conditions the iridologist thinks need attention. Some iridologists who are trained in therapies such as osteopathy or reflexology may be able to treat their patients following diagnosis. Others must refer patients to the most appropriate practitioner, commonly a homeopath or an acupuncturist. Some herbal and naturopathic practitioners also use this form of diagnosis in conjunction with their own methods, because they find that it has the advantage of being easy and painless for the patient.

## Massage

Massage is not a complete therapy in itself, but forms part of several other therapies, notably physiotherapy, chiropractic and reflexology. The massage used in acupuncture is called Shiatsu and is slightly different.

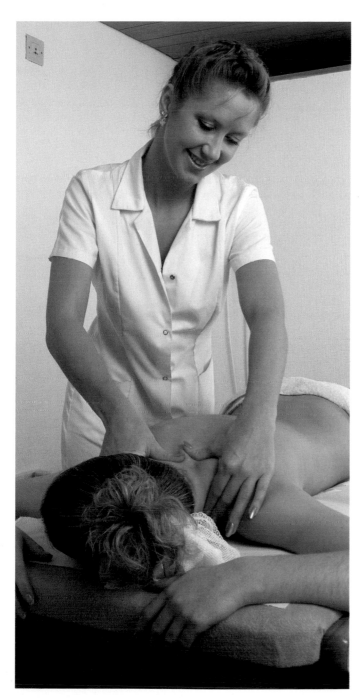

*Massage is an ancient therapy which supports and complements almost all other forms of medicine. On its own, it helps combat stress and promote beneficial relaxation.*

Massage consists of rubbing, kneading, pummelling or pressing on the muscles and soft tissues of the body. The main aim of massage is to relax tense muscles and tone up the body generally, and it is often used by professional sports people and musicians, whose occupations involve them in continual muscular stress. It is a useful complementary treatment to homeopathy, reducing harmful levels of tension in both mind and body.

**Naturopathy**
Naturopathy is not so much a system of healing as a way of healthy living. A naturopath believes that many of the illnesses we suffer from are due to the accumulation of poisonous waste materials in the body. They maintain that the body's natural force will do its own job of healing if the patient detoxifies the system. Ridding the body of poisonous wastes is accomplished by a combination of closely supervised fasting, colonic irrigation and enemas, supported by careful dieting. Naturopaths believe that the body will cure itself once the waste substances are eliminated, and that signs and symptoms are indications that the body is trying to rid itself of the cause of disease.

Once the period of fasting is over the patient is recommended to follow a diet designed to prevent any recurrence of the previous illness. The exact diet varies from patient to patient, and from naturopath to naturopath, but probably includes the avoidance of stimulants such as tea, coffee and alcohol, and such foods as white sugar and sweets. Naturopaths often recommend vitamin and mineral supplements to the diet to counteract imbalances that may have occurred over the years through bad eating habits, or by consuming over-processed and artificial food that is lacking in natural goodness.

The homeopathic view of dietary supplements is that they may sometimes by needed when a person has been unable to assimilate vitamins and minerals from their normal food intake, or has been following a deficient diet. But – and it is a big but – homeopaths consider that even if such supplements are needed as a temporary measure, they should not be continued indefinitely. If they are, the body may become dependent on them and fail to do its proper job of absorbing the substances from a normal, well-balanced diet. In such a case homeopathic medication can help the patient's metabolism to make the best use of the food.

Some homeopathic practitioners also practice naturopathy. Often they do not prescribe any homeopathic medicines until their patients have first followed a detoxifying diet. Practitioners are then able to observe how many signs and symptoms have improved, and to what extent, simply as a result of the change of diet. At that point they reconsider the patient's condition to see what kind of homeopathic treatment is now needed, and what remedy is indicated.

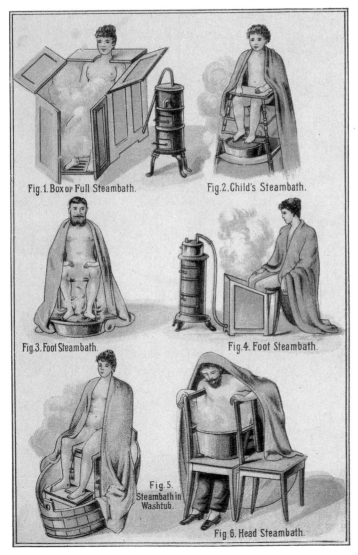

Fig.1. Box or Full Steambath.

Fig.2. Child's Steambath.

Fig.3. Foot Steambath.

Fig.4. Foot Steambath.

Fig.5. Steambath in Washtub.

Fig 6. Head Steambath.

*Steam baths and various kinds of steam bathing were hailed as wonder cures in the Victorian era. Unfortunately, the hot, damp atmosphere helped spread germs and so such bathing was not always as beneficial as it was claimed.*

*Osteopathy maintains
that most disorders result
from a structural fault in
the body's nervous,
muscular or skeletal
system, and has
perfected techniques to
restore these systems to
their proper form.*

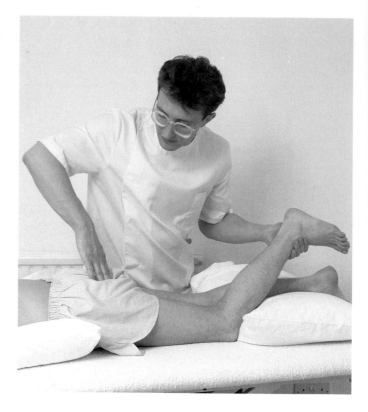

### Osteopathy

Like chiropractic, osteopathy is directed at manipulating the
bones and joints to correct any misplacement. It was
founded in 1874 by Dr Andrew Taylor Still (1828-1917), an
American physician. He served as a doctor with the Union
armies during the American Civil War.

Taylor and his successors believed that the skeleton and
its attached muscles relate to all other organs of the body
even to the circulation of the blood. Consequently musculo-skeletal disturbances can have a profound effect on the
rest of the body, even producing signs and symptoms of
disease. Osteopaths think that misplacement of the bones,
particularly of the vertebrae in the spine, can affect the
nerves, which become stretched or misplaced and consequently send false messages around the body. Taylor coined
the phrase 'osteopathic lesion' to describe the kind of local-
ized disorders he thought could be caused by injury, disease,
or nervous tension.

In the United States osteopaths are recognized as physicians. They qualify after six or seven years of university and specialized training, which results in graduation with a doctorate in osteopathy. In Britain few osteopaths have formal medical training outside that provided by a specialized osteopathic training institution.

Most osteopathic patients have back troubles of one kind or another. As with chiropractic, the services of an osteopath may well be indicated if there is distortion or misalignment of any joint.

## Psychotherapy

Somebody suffering from long-term depression, anxiety, mental or emotional problems, or a personality disorder, may consider going to a psychotherapist, a psychoanalyst or a clinical psychologist. All these people are concerned with the treatment and prevention of mental illness. They work with patients regularly over a long period of time, trying to help resolve some difficulties in their lives. These difficulties may be deep-rooted, having their origins in some unpleasant experience (possibly as long ago as childhood), which has been thrust into the subconscious. Psychotherapy may help to liberate these forgotten fears or anxieties.

Psychiatry, which includes psychotherapy and psychoanalysis, is a branch of the medical profession. In the UK and the United States psychiatrists are qualified physicians who have gone on to specialize in the subject. Clinical psychologists are concerned with abnormal human behaviour; they are attached to the medical profession, but their training is independent of normal medical training. They study psychology at university, taking higher degrees such as MA (Master of Arts) or PhD (Doctor of Philosophy, a reserach degree), followed by in-service training in a psychological clinic.

It often helps to talk over one's problems with someone else; psychotherapy is a very specialized form of such 'talking over'. Many patterns of behaviour that inhibit a patient's reaction to other people have their origin in a response to earlier experiences. Often people try to forget unpleasant episodes from their past, but such repression often results in a false picture of themselves and their characters, and negative attitudes to life. It can take a lot of work, energy, and willingness to change to free the mind from repressions and blocks.

Homeopathic remedies can help people mentally and emotionally, as well as with physical symptoms that may arise as a result of the chronic ill-effects of some unhappiness or pattern of behaviour. But in certain cases some form of psychotherapy is needed in addition to the medication, to help patients change negative attitudes, to more freely express their own natures, and explore their potential to the full. As Hahnemann wrote in his *Organon:*

*'One should not overlook [the patient's] emotional and mental disposition, to ascertain whether it might be an impediment to the treatment and whether psychological attention might be necessary to guide, encourage, or change it.'*

### Reflexology

Reflexology is a form of therapy that seeks to restore health and fitness through foot massage. It is a very old form of therapy, practised by the ancient Chinese and Egyptians, but developed in its modern form in the 1920s and 1930s. Reflexologists believe there are 'channels of energy' that terminate in the feet, but are connected to the various vital organs of the body. The exact part of the foot that is manipulated or massaged depends on what organ the reflexologist is trying to treat. An important part of the therapy is making patients relax, and because tension is a factor in many illnesses this can do only good.

*Reflexology is based on the idea that each part of the foot corresponds with a particular part or organ of the body and that massage or stimulation of the relevant foot area can promote health in the corresponding part of the body. Here the big toe, which relates to the head and pituitary gland, is being stretched and compressed.*

## Yoga

Yoga is a system of mental and physical exercise, which aims to create a healthy mind in a healthy body. It is derived from ancient Hindu religious traditions. As practised in the West, it aims to improve bodily health by relaxing the mind through meditation, while relieving tensions through exercises, and encouraging correct breathing.

Yoga is thought to be particularly suitable for treating stress-caused disorders, and homeopaths occasionally recommend it to their patients with this in mind. It has been found beneficial in many cases of asthma, arthritis, backache, and hypertension. Its greatest value in maintaining health is its capacity to induce complete mental and physical relaxation.

*Yoga is an ancient therapy, part exercise, part self-massage, part meditation. Beginners can be helped to achieve the correct position if they are not flexible enough to begin with.*

# 7

# FOUNDATIONS
# OF HOMEOPATHY

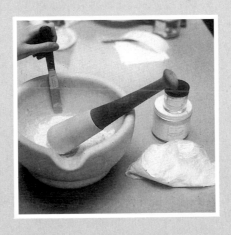

Christian Friedrich Samuel Hahnemann was born in 1755 at Meissen in the Electorate of Saxony (now part of East Germany). As a boy Hahnemann was good at his studies and he had a talent for languages. His developing interest in science and medicine led him to further studies. In 1775 he went to Leipzig, where he spent several years in training and study, followed by an apprenticeship to Dr Josef von Quarin, a court physician in Vienna.

Like most students, Hahnemann had to find work to support himself while he studied. His skill in languages – he spoke eight fluently – brought him work as a translator for scientific publishers. For two years he was librarian to the governor of Transylvania, then part of Hungary. While there he was able to continue his studies and to earn money by translation. He finally received his doctorate in medicine in 1779 from the University of Erlangen, now in West Germany.

Hahnemann spent several years travelling from place to place in the various German states of that time, practising as a physician. During this time he became more and more disturbed by the medical practices of his day. Doctors often used crude doses of dangerous substances such as mercury, arsenic, opium, and white hellebore. Large doses of herbs were administered as purgatives, and some physicians used mixtures of up to a dozen strong herbs or other substances as specifics for various ailments. The descriptions in literature of fairground quacks and their cure-all potions were merely extreme examples of this way of thinking. Bloodletting to relieve symptoms was still commonly practised, and leeches were applied to the skin to suck blood for the same purpose. Maggots were applied to wounds to eat the pus that oozed from them.

### Research and experiment

Settling in Leipzig in 1789, Hahnemann observed numerous signs in his patients indicating the poisonous effects of the medicines then in use. He was alarmed by what he found. Although he had a considerable reputation as a physician, he virtually gave up practising medicine for a time in 1796. Instead he supported himself and his wife largely by translating foreign medical books, while pursuing his own researches. Much of his time was spent observing and experimenting with methods that might be used to cure people, without being as damaging to their general health as

*Whatever you can do, or dream you can, begin it. Boldness has genius, power and magic in it.*

Johann von Goethe

*Leeching, letting blood via the natural bloodsucking activities of the leech, was once an indispensable tool of physicians. Bloodletting was thought to help high blood pressure and let poisons escape from the body. Unfortunately, even more poisons were introduced to the body, as the operation was not usually accompanied by any form of antiseptic. Here, leeching is taking place in a bath house; the cross-infection is too awful to contemplate.*

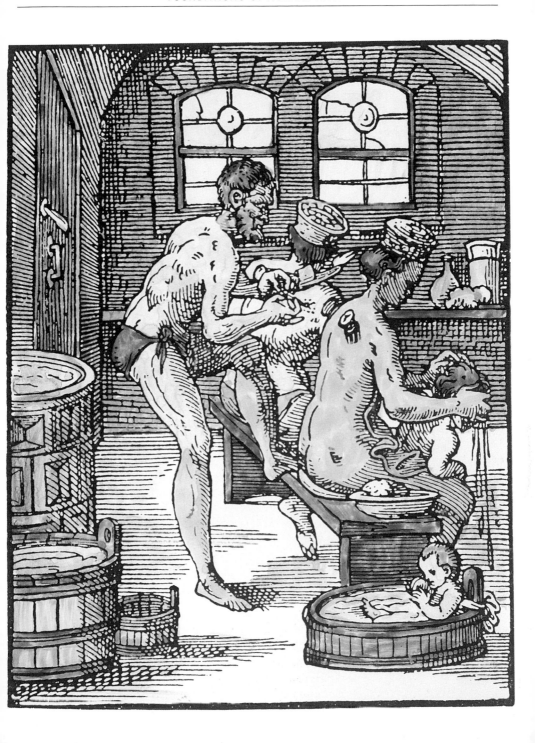

were many of the treatments then commonly in use.

Several observations led Hahnemann to start developing his homeopathic theories. He noticed that if a person with a chronic condition temporarily developed an acute illness which resembled the chronic one, it seemed to relieve the chronic signs and symptoms while it lasted. He also made note of the symptoms of poisoning induced by many of the chemicals and herbs used in medicine, especially when given in large quantities or over a prolonged period of time.

Through his studies, and his work on translating foreign medical texts, Hahnemann came across the then newly-discovered remedy, cinchona – also known as Peruvian bark or Jesuit's bark, from the place and the people who discovered it – which is now the source of quinine and other related drugs. Doctors were starting to use Peruvian bark for the treatment of intermittent fevers, such as swamp fevers and illnesses of the malarial kind, which were then common in Europe. Hahnemann had himself frequently needed to treat them, notably during his stay in Transylvania.

At the time Hahnemann was translating a *Materia Medica* (a work detailing the substances used in medicines) by the Scottish physician William Cullen (1710-1790), a professor of medicine in Glasgow and Edinburgh who had a wide reputation as a teacher. Cullen's book gave an explanation of the action of quinine in treating malaria, but his reasoning did not satisfy Hahnemann.

Seeking an answer to this problem, he was inspired to experiment on himself by taking doses of Peruvian bark until he produced all the symptoms of intermittent fever. This historic experiment convinced Hahnemann that the reason why Peruvian bark cured intermittent fever was because it had the power to create a similar fever in a healthy person. From this the Law of Similars was born.

### Similia similibus curantur

Following this experiment, Hahnemann formulated his theory that substances should be 'proved' on healthy persons in order to ascertain their true medicinal properties. At the same time he developed his theory of *similia similibus curantur* ('like cures like'): a substance that produced symptoms in a healthy person could, he believed, also cure similar symptoms in a sick person.

Because Hahnemann was concerned about the poisonous nature of so many medical substances then in use, he

*Belladonna, or deadly nightshade, contains the alkaloids hyoscyamine, hyoscine and atropine.*

decided to experiment to discover the smallest amount of a drug that could be given, and still be curative. From these experiments he developed the theory of dilution and succussion (vigorous shaking) in preparing his medicines.

From then on Hahnemann began experimenting with those poisonous substances which he knew would produce signs and symptoms that would be similar to those of diseases. For example, he found that people who swallowed the berries of deadly nightshade (*Atropa belladonna*), which contains the alkaloid atropine, developed signs and symptoms similar to those of scarlet fever, including redness of the throat, a 'strawberry' tongue, high fever, flushed complexion and delirium In those days fashionable women used white arsenic (*Arsenicum alba*) to whiten the skin; this dangerous substance could produce chronic debility, weakness, nausea, vomiting and diarrhoea. Mercury, at that time commonly used in the treatment of syphilis, can produce inflammation of the gums, kidney disorders and the condition of tremor known as 'hatter's shakes' commonly suffered by the makers of felt hats, because mercurous nitrate was used in their production.

To test his theories, Hahnemann made homeopathic dilutions of various substances. He gave repeated doses of these homeopathic dilutions to healthy volunteers, recruited

*Alice's demented host at the tea party was no figment of Lewis Carroll's imagination. The 'felting' of hats involved the use of mercury which is know to poison the nervous system. Unprotected workers were slowly poisoned and suffered nerve damage which resulted in uncontrollable shaking and ultimately madness. 'Mad as a hatter' entered the language, where it has remained a semantic relic of an outlawed industrial process.*

from among his family, friends and medical students. The volunteers were not told what substances they were proving, and to ensure that no outside substances interfered with the experiments they were forbidden to smoke, or take strongly flavoured foods or alcohol. Hahnemann carried on with the doses until these 'provers', as they were called, began to produce sets of signs and symptoms similar to those observed in cases of poisoning, as well as many others not revealed in poisoning.

Hahnemann took careful note of all the signs and symptoms produced, comparing those in different volunteers. In this way he gradually built up a picture of some 67 remedies, which he tried out homeopathic doses on various patients with similar symptoms.

By 1810 he had published a description of the medicines he

had proved in a *Materia Medica* and an explanation of his theories – the *Organon*. This gave details of his method of working. Writing in the *Organon* he noted that: 'The curative virtues of medicines thus depend on their symptoms being similar to those of the disease, but stronger.' From this, he argued, a disease could be destroyed completely only by such medicines. These initial theories Hahnemann continued to develop and confirm, through experiment and clinical practice, for 53 years until his death in 1843.

One of his earliest and greatest successes came after the Battle of Leipzig in 1813, in which the combined armies of Austria, Prussia, Russia and Sweden defeated the French army of Napoleon I. Nearly 100,000 soldiers were killed or wounded, but even more deadly was a virulent epidemic of typhoid. Hahnemann treated 180 cases, and lost just one patient. This victory over disease greatly enhanced his reputation, and that of homeopathy.

### Earlier approaches to homeopathy

Hahnemann did not invent homeopathy completely out of the blue. There were certain approaches to healing that had been used from ancient times which were partly homeopathic in their applications, although neither subtle nor scientific.

One of the most fanciful was the so-called 'Doctrine of Signatures', in which substances were used as medicines because of their fancied resemblance to the affected part of the body. For example, a walnut, out of its shell, looks superficially like the brain, so it was given to treat brain disorders. The lichen lungwort (*Lobaria pulmonaria*) gets its name because it was thought to look like a diseased lung, as were the spotted leaves of the herb *Pulmonaria officinalis*, also called lungwort. Both the lichen and the herb were used to treat tuberculosis.

Other folk remedies included some simple actions that a few people still take today, such as wrapping the prickly side of a bramble leaf around a finger that has a thorn in it, in order to draw the thorn out; or rubbing the feet with snow to relieve chilblains. The Romans used to beat themselves with stinging nettles to relieve the pain and swelling of rheumatism. Another old folk remedy involved drinking a tea made of scalded bees to promote the flow of urine, after it was noticed that some victims of bee-stings developed swellings and retention of urine. All these strange remedies were a groping towards the basic idea of homeopathy, that 'like cures like'.

A striking example of 'like cures like' occurred in Hahnemann's own practice. One of his friends, an artist, was suffering severely from weakness, and had become indifferent to his family. Hahnemann spent some time with his friend in his studio. He noticed that from time to time the artist would suck his brush. He was painting with sepia ink, made from the brown-black juice of the cuttlefish, which was then in common use. Hahnemann took the ink and made a homeopathic dilution of it, which he then administered to his friend. It produced an improvement in his condition.

One of Hahnemann's greatest inspirations was his decision to dilute the remedies in the very specific way that he did. He added one part of the mother tincture – the basic potency of the drug – to nine parts of water and alcohol, or milk sugar (lactose), or one part of medicine to ninety-nine parts of the other substance. All modern potencies are still prepared according to this principle.

In Hahnemann's day it was customary for doctors to study and practice pharmacy, and Hahnemann spent a lot of time in his laboratory experimenting with substances before he finalized his homeopathic views of medicine. He strongly believed that physicians should make up their own remedies. This view brought him into conflict with the apothecaries in Germany, who saw their livelihood threatened. Today, only a few physicians who are also qualified pharmacists can dispense their own medicines. So most homeopaths obtain their remedies from specialized homeopathic pharmacies. Some of these are listed in the reference chapter of this book.

**The miasm theory**
After Hahnemann had been developing his theories and working with patients for some time, prescribing the remedies most similar to their signs and symptoms, he observed that some of his chronically-ill patients were simply not improving. From this he formulated a new theory: that some chronic disease is the result of an underlying one, which he called a miasm. (A miasm means a trace of a scent that is left: for example, the residual perfume of flowers that have just been removed from a room.) Today, we regard such underlying diseases as a hereditary trait, handed down

from generation to generation through genetic coding.

Hahnemann saw many cases of chronic disease following on from the suppression of skin eruptions – 'the itch', as he called them – or after treatment with mercury and other powerful drugs for syphilis and gonorrhoea. Where the apparently similar remedy was not improving the patient's condition, he decided to give a remedy connected with the apparent disease, the miasm, that had either been suppressed or inherited.

The basic and most universal miasm Hahnemann called *psora* – from a Greek word meaning 'itch' – which he considered to be the father and mother of all disease in mankind. For this he made a remedy from the scabies vesicle. This was Hahnemann's first *nosode* remedy – that is, one made from a disease product.

*Psora* is expressed as a slowing down of the system. People suffering from the psoric miasm display a lot of anxiety, and tend to be introverted and repressed. They have a feeling that somehow they have 'lost out' in life, that they are separated or alienated from society, and some patients may even have a crisis of identity. They tend to be hesitant and slow thinking, although with a good memory. They fear failure and poverty, and have an underlying dread that 'something will happen'. Such patients have a lack of vital heat, in other words, they are chilly people. They are likely to be at their best in the morning, worse by midday, and slow down noticeably by the evening – although they may become mentally active and anxious when it is time to go to sleep. Such people often display dry skin eruptions, and suffer from slow degenerative diseases.

Hahnemann described two other miasms, both originating in venereal disease, which were sometimes coupled with *psora*. These he called the *sycotic* miasm and the *syphilitic* miasm.

The *sycotic* miasm is related to gonorrhoea. This venereal disease has been known since prehistoric times, although it was not recognized as a separate disease from syphilis until 1790. In the Middle Ages there were plagues of gonorrhoea which affected a large proportion of the population of Europe. The *syphilitic* miasm is related to syphilis. This disease became rife in Europe soon after the return of Christopher Columbus and his men from the New World in 1493, and for many years it was thought that the disease originated among the American Indians. However, some

*Christopher Columbus (1451-1506) who opened up the New World unwittingly became a disease vector, as he and his crew carried diseases to and from the newly discovered lands and old Europe.*

medical historians now think that it had existed in Europe before Columbus's day, but had been classified as and confused with leprosy. Others think it was introduced into Europe from Africa, where a disease called yaws, caused by a bacterium similar to that which causes syphilis, was common. In any case the disease seems to have changed its character during the sixteenth-century. But whatever the origin of venereal diseases, it would seem from Hahnemann's case notes that a great many of the middle-class people of Europe suffered from some form of venereal infection at one time or another.

Hahnemann regarded other miasms as coming from a combination of these basic miasms; thus the tubercular miasm arose from a combination of the psoric miasm with one of the other two, and the cancerous miasm from a combination of all three. When a well-indicated remedy failed to act, Hahnemann would analyze the case and see which of the miasms appeared to be dominant. He would then give a miasmic remedy, generally though not always a nosode. Based on Hahnemann's practice, the remedies chosen for *psora* are *Psorinum*, derived from the scabies vesicle, or *Sulphur* or *Graphites*. For *sycosis* the remedies are *Medorrhinum*, derived from gonorrhoeal pus, *Thuja occidentalis* (from the North American evergreen 'tree of life'), or *Natrum sulphuricum* (Glauber's salt, sodium sulphate), two remedies that have a great effect on skin troubles. For the *syphilitic* miasm the treatment is *Syphilinum*, a remedy derived from the syphilis bacterium or *Mercurium*.

Hahnemann expressed his theories about miasms in his book *Chronic Diseases*. They met with persistent opposition from allopathic doctors, and even from some of his own followers. Indeed, the theory of miasms still attracts controversy today. It must be stressed that if people are suffering from a miasm it does not necessarily mean that they or their immediate relatives have actually had the causative disease, but that the miasms are traits in our collective inheritance. The consequences of venereal disease are deeply rooted, whether we like the idea or not.

### Hahnemann's later life

As Hahnemann's reputation grew steadily, opposition to his theories also mounted, not only from his old enemies the apothecaries, but also from orthodox doctors in Leipzig. Then in 1820 one of his most distinguished patients, Prince Karl Philipp von Schwarzenberg (the Austrian field-marshal who had led the Allied armies to victory over Napoleon at the Battle of Leipzig seven years earlier) died following a stroke. Hahnemann's enemies seized their chance to discredit him. They burned his writings and medicines in public, and subjected him to public ridicule. The following year he accepted an invitation from Grand Duke Ferdinand of Anhalt to move to Ctthen (now Ktthen in East Germany), where he remained for the next 14 years. Following the death of his wife in 1830, he married a young Frenchwoman and, in 1835, moved to Paris where it would be easier for his many followers throughout Europe to consult him. He died there, aged 88.

His widow, Melanie Hahneman, became well-known as a homeopath in her own right, and towards the end of her life was awarded a doctorate in medicine – despite the hostility of many French doctors. At that time and, indeed, for many years afterwards, medicine was still considered a male preserve. Following Melanie Hahnemann's lead, however, homeopathic medical schools were among the first to admit female students.

### Developments in homeopathy

An important difference between homeopathy and allopathy is that the homeopathic principles for treatment and cure laid down by Hahnemann nearly two hundred years ago are still relevant today – although some of his theories have been amplified and developed. With allopathic medicine the ideas and drugs that are used change almost from year to year, and today's orthodoxy becomes tomorrow's heresy. There even seem to be fashions in the prescription of medicines, which may be partly due to advertising pressure put on physicians by drug companies.

The first two countries in which homeopathy was practised were Germany and France, and there are still homeopathic practitioners in both countries today. Not all of them follow the true teachings of Hahnemann, however. New movements to improve the standard of homeopathic practice are developing throughout Europe. Many practising homeopaths, including allopathic doctors who have been converted to homeopathic medicines, attend post-graduate seminars. The study of homeopathic theory, *Materia Medica* and clinical practice is a vast one, and no practitioner ever stops learning.

From France and Germany, homeopathy was taken to Britain and the United States in the early nineteenth century. It spread from Britain throughout the old British Empire, while from the United States it was taken to Canada and Central America.

The physician who introduced homeopathy to Britain was an Edinburgh-qualified doctor called Dr Frederick Hervey Foster Quin. He went to Italy in 1821 as medical attendant to the Duchess of Devonshire and while there met a disciple of Hahnemann, Dr Georg Necker, who interested him in the subject. Dr Quin decided to visit Leipzig and learn more about homeopathy from Samuel Hahnemann himself.

In 1827, Quin returned to England as physician to Prince Leopold of Saxe-Coburg, uncle of the future Queen, Victoria and her husband, Prince Albert. Quin held the post

*Dr Frederick Hervey Foster QW Quin, caricatured in* Vanity Fair. *Dr Quin worked with Samuel Hahnemann, and introduced homeopathy to Great Britain.*

until 1829, entering general practice in London in 1832. Because of his reputation and his connection with Prince Leopold, he soon numbered many members of the aristocracy among his patients.

Like Hahnemann in Germany, however, Quin and his ideas were vigorously opposed by orthodox doctors, several of whom denounced him as a quack. Ignoring these attacks, Quin founded the British Homeopathic Society in 1844, now known as the Faculty of Homeopathy.

## Homeopathy in the United States

The nineteenth-century persecution of homeopathic practitioners in Britain, and criticism of homeopathy generally, was matched by similar opposition in the United States. A leading homeopath in the United States was Dr Constantine Hering (1800-1880), who was born in Saxony. When still a medical student at the University of Leipzig, he was asked to write an article attacking homeopathy. He undertook the task with enthusiasm, but his researches led him to become a convert to the new medicine. Settling in the United States in 1833, Hering established a practice in Philadelphia, Pennsylvania. In 1844 he and his colleagues founded the American Institute of Homeopathy.

Three years later, as a direct result of this move, 250 orthodox doctors meeting in Philadelphia founded the American Medical Association (the AMA). At once the AMA and the American drug companies began a campaign to try to eliminate homeopathic practitioners, and at the beginning of the twentieth century they almost succeeded. In his book *The Divided Legacy*, the medical historian Harris Coulter (whose wife is a leading homeopathic practitioner in the United States) has vividly described the struggle:

> 'For sixty years the AMA was vehemently hostile to the homeopaths. Regardless of the fact that many of the latter had graduated from Harvard, Dartmouth, Pennsylvania, and other leading medical schools they were refused admittance to the orthodox medical societies. Professional consultation was punished by ostracism and expulsion from the regular medical societies.'

In 1912 the American Institute of Homeopaths offered to take part in a controlled investigation of homeopaths and its medicines. The AMA refused the offer.

### Changing views on traditional medicine

The World Health Organization (WHO) produced a report in 1985 entitled *Consultation on approaches for policy development for traditional health practitioners, including traditional birth attendants*. It says:

> '*We respect the knowledge of traditional health practitioners . . . They are the richest source of community health care. We should remember that we want them as allies.*'

The report describes the situation in several countries where there are both traditional practitioners and physicians trained in orthodox Western medicine. It says that unless the traditional practitioners can be integrated into national health care systems, many countries will never be able to provide adequate health care for all their people.

Among the report's recommendations is a proposal that the Chinese model of health care should be followed on a wider scale. In the Chinese system there is mutual recognition of the different systems practised, and respect by practitioners of one system for the work of those of another. Traditional practitioner's receive some training in orthodox Western medicine, and ordinary physicians gain some knowledge of traditional methods. Hospitals of one system have departments that deal with the medical methods of the other.

An important light on changing contemporary views of alternative medicine has been shed in several articles by Dr Stephen Fulder. Dr Fulder is a biochemist who now runs a research consultancy on complementary medicine. Writing in *Impact of Science on Society*, No 143, he said:

> '*The historical roots of traditional and modern Western medicine are the same, but during the past century these systems diverged. Modern medicine became dominant, outlawing traditional systems and denouncing them as quackery. In recent years there has been a resurgence of interest in traditional systems, and in the United Kingdom particularly a remarkable change in attitude among younger doctors. Many now learn traditional techniques themselves or refer patients to traditional practitioners. This trend should be encouraged, and could save much of the tremendous expense of modern medicine.*'

*HRH Prince Charles, the Prince of Wales whose interest in and promotion of complementary medicine is shared by his mother and the rest of the Royal Family.*

The Prince of Wales, a past president of the British Medical Association, told members of the association (as reported in *The Times* of 30 June 1983):

> '*What is taken for today's orthodoxy is probably going to be tomorrow's convention . . . account has to be taken of those sometimes long-neglected complementary methods of medicine.*'

## Complementary medicine in Western Europe

The position of complementary medicine in Western Europe is very uncertain and confused. For example, homeopathy, acupuncture, chiropractic, herbalism and naturopathy are legal in the United Kingdom, but illegal in Belgium, Italy, Jersey, and Spain. The Netherlands has just changed its laws to make them legal; formerly they were illegal, but completely tolerated. The Scandinavian countries and West Germany recognize them, but with restrictions on who can practise. Chiropractic is legal in France and Switzerland; the others are generally illegal, but in France many doctors have taken up homeopathy, acupuncture and herbalism.

People vote with their feet; even where complementary medical systems are officially banned, millions of people seek homeopathic and other consultations. The law had to be changed in the Netherlands because 18 per cent of the Dutch people were using complementary medicine. Many of them consult homeopaths, and it is now possible for a Dutch person to obtain homeopathic treatment, through the Dutch health service, from practitioners who have been trained solely in the homeopathic tradition.

Stephen Fulder has pointed out that the wise use of complementary medicine could save much unnecessary use of medical resources and hospital beds. He recommends that money could be saved if homeopathic practitioners, whose period of training is shorter – and therefore cheaper – than that of orthodox medical practitioners should receive support from orthodox doctors, especially in the field of diagnosis. He adds:

*'It seems to me that the developed Western countries would do well to consider incorporating some of the recommendations of the World Health Organization for developing countries in their own health care policies.'*

In Britain, the Netherlands and some other parts of Europe several homeopathic colleges have been established in recent years for training physicians in homeopathic medicine.

## Homeopathy in the United States and elsewhere

The practice of homeopathy is still illegal in some parts of the United States, although this situation is changing rapidly. In Argentina, Brazil, Chile, India, Mexico, and the Soviet Union homeopathy has continued to be practised by people trained purely as homeopathic physicians or as homeopathic practitioners, or by orthodox doctors who have changed direction and gone on to study homeopathy in depth.

## Present-day approaches to homeopathy

Samuel Hahnemann continually revised his *Organon* throughout his long working life. The sixth and final revision was lost for a while, and not rediscovered and published until 1921, 78 years after his death. This means that his last definitive ideas on the ways to use remedies and

---

**Homeopathy and the law** Although homeopathy is legal in the UK and USA, it enjoys variable legal status in Europe.

- In France and the Netherlands, it is illegal, but totally tolerated. (In the Netherlands, the law is about to be changed.)
- In Scandinavia, it is legal but hedged with restrictions.
- In West Germany and Luxembourg, it is illegal unless the homeopath is a *heilpraktiker* (non medical practitioner).
- In Belgium, Italy, Spain and Jersey, it is illegal.
- In Switzerland, it is illegal except in the canton of Appenzell.

This gives homeopathy the same status as acupuncture and herbalism.

their potencies were not discovered until then. His later case notes were not worked through and analyzed until the 1980s; Rima Handley, PhD, RS Hom., has edited them (*Hahnemann's Later Prescribing*; Beaconsfield Press 1988).

As a result many of Hahnemann's followers developed their own ideas on the proper use of remedies. Today there are several main approaches to case analysis and prescribing by masters of the science of homeopathy. However, they all hold in common Hahnemann's basic tenets – in particular the principle of one remedy at a time, except in the case of acute emergencies or miasmatic blocks.

## Analysis and treatment: the Hahnemannian method

A number of different approaches to treatment seem to be effective: the first being the Hahnemannian 'symptom and miasm' method of prescribing. In this method the homeopathic practitioner prescribes the first remedy on the basis of the obvious signs and symptoms of disease, plus any other signs that might need to be taken into account – such as sleep patterns or food cravings.

Suppose a patient complains of a combination of the following symptoms: arthritic pains in the limbs that have a drawing, tearing nature, and are relieved by the warmth of bed and – strangely enough – by damp weather; neuralgic pains in the feet making walking unsteady and even producing a tendency to fall; cramping as a result of these symptoms; warts on the hands or face; and involuntary emission of urine when sneezing or coughing at night. As the first stage of treatment the practitioner would prescribe *Causticum*, based on these symptoms, without delving into the patient's past history to ascertain a possible long-term cause – perhaps from grief, fright or suppressed emotions.

Knowing that *Causticum* is a remedy that is applicable to all the miasms, the practitioner would see that the patient needing this remedy would also be likely to have one or more miasms active in them at some level. He or she would therefore consider that remedies dealing with miasms would need to be taken in to account as 'intercurrent' (simultaneous) treatment in this case.

The presence of warts would suggest starting with an intercurrent remedy for the sycotic miasm, such as *Medorhinum*. Hahnemann himself often started a case with a remedy appropriate to *psoric* (non-venereal) miasm, either *Sulphur* or *Graphites*, and then went on to give the remedy

indicated by the patient's signs and symptoms. Otherwise
he initially prescribed the remedy indicated by the signs and
symptoms, and gave an anti-miasmatic remedy as an intercurrent.

### Past and present
The second main approach is to take the whole case – that is,
not only to study all the present and past signs and symptoms, but also to look beyond them to see what was happening in the patient's life before the emergence of any
mental, emotional, or physical manifestations of disease.
This method puts more emphasis in the case analysis on apparent causes of chronic trouble. Often, these causes are
grief, emotional upset, or shock. Prolonged physical stress
– such as intensive studying, exposure to the elements, or
hard physical work in a damp place – can also profoundly
affect health and vitality. Practitioners using this approach
insist that any remedy they give must have among its
'symptom pictures' the apparent cause of the weakening of
the system, before the pathological signs and symptoms
appeared.

### Layers of disease
The third main approach considers very much the layers or
stages of morbidity (disease) that have built up during the
whole lifetime of the patient. Starting with the present picture given by the signs and symptoms, the practitioner
works backward, maybe from one remedy to another, hop-
ing to remove the different layers of morbidity as one
removes layers from an onion. This school of thought
declares that one must remove one layer of disease at a time
and not dig too deeply at the start. In this way the practitioner can avoid any aggravation of symptoms during the
healing process, and comes eventually to the constitutional
remedy which helps to keep the patient healthy in the long
term.

### The psychoanalytical approach
The fourth approach is psychoanalytical. It has been developed by such men as Paschal de Pascero from Argentina
and Edward C. Whitmont, a psychoanalyst and a disciple of
Carl Gustav Jung (1875-1961), the Swiss physician who developed analytical psychology. Practitioners following this
approach spend time not only on looking at the cause and

effect of mind on body – and vice versa – but also on considering non-causality (possible links between apparently unrelated factors) as a scientific principle suitable for a better understanding of nature.

## Personality and physical problems

So we come to a paradox in homeopathy: does the personality type produce the physical signs and symptoms? Does possession of the same physical type and predisposition produce the personality type? Or are these just occurring at the same time and not in fact caused by each other? Practitioners who prescribe according to the psychoanalytical approach

*Carl Gustav Jung (1875-1961) the Swiss psychiatrist who pioneered the theory of an archetypal unconsciousness which we all share.*

concentrate on discovering the underlying conflict in the patient, and prescribe the appropriate remedy for this conflict.

Since homeopathic practitioners are constantly adding to their *Materia Medica* from clinical experience, they can supplement it according to what is learned of personality types. Today we understand more about the different stages and development of the personality. Some practitioners approach the question of personality type along the lines advocated by the Austrian psychiatrist Alfred Adler (1870-1937), founder of the school of individual psychology. According to Adler, a patient is thought to suffer from a basic inner conflict, followed by a stage of containment within that person. If there is deep stress, the person goes through a struggle or a breakdown, in which the (previously contained) original conflicts take over and cause what is called a mental breakdown. Practitioners who follow this school have seen that where they understand the essence of the personality type accurately, a remedy that fits that type often works well, whether or not it fits the physical signs and symptoms. Possibly this works only if the physical pathology is within the range of the remedy, although this may not have shown up when the remedy was originally proved.

**Mexican developments**
Another approach was developed by a Dr Ortega, of Mexico. In this, all the abnormal signs and symptoms are analyzed as being either hyperfunctioning (over-functioning), hypofunctioning (under-functioning), or dis-energetic functioning (energy turned in on itself and self-consuming). This modern terminology fits with Hahnemann's original three miasms. Hyperfunctioning equates with sycotic miasm; hypofunctioning with psoric miasm; and dis-energetic functioning with syphilitic miasm.

Practitioners who adopt this approach insist that the remedy must be relevant to the miasm that is uppermost in the patient at that time, and they prescribe a miasmic remedy first, before one based on the patient's signs and symptoms. Some of these practitioners treat expectant mothers during the later months of pregnancy with remedies that pertain to all three miasms, believing that this treatment will help to combat any inherited weakness in the child before it is born.

## Fundamental constitution

Finally, there is a sixth approach, in which practitioners base their prescribing on a study of the fundamental constitution of the patient – as it was when he or she was a child before being overlaid by adult pathology. The practitioners decide what remedy the patient would have needed as a child; then select a remedy that would suit the original constitution.

This works initially when the case is simple – that is, the patient has a basically strong constitution, and has remained the same constitutional type all through life, although perhaps developing different signs and symptoms from time to time. However, where the signs and symptoms suggest another remedy, on top of the constitutional type, then the constitutional remedy has only a limited effect and may not be able to clear up some of the physical pathology until a remedy for that particular disease layer has been given first.

## Appropriate prescribing

The followers of all these approaches to homeopathic prescribing have very good results, but they may miss out on some if they are too dogmatic. The 'approach of appropriate prescribing' uses different ways of analyzing a case and prescribing for it according to the level of disease in the patient at that time. In other words, sometimes it is important to deal with miasmic blocks first, sometimes not.

Hahnemann's later case notes indicates that his experiments were concerned with finding the most appropriate and gentle way of obtaining an improvement in a patient's condition. For some he prescribed just one remedy; for others alternating remedies – that is, one medicine at one time of day and a second at another time, or perhaps alternate remedies on alternate days. If an acute condition arose during treatment, he prescribed a different remedy to treat that condition. He also gave an intercurrent miasmic remedy, perhaps a fortnight or a month after the first remedy, to help clear up the ill-effects of previous suppression. Never at any time did he prescribe several remedies mixed together (polypharmacy).

Finally, here is a tribute from a patient who wrote after taking a homeopathic remedy for the first time:

> *'I felt both astonished and intellectually satisfied to see what a smooth and pure mechanism this form of treatment is, if the dose is administered accurately at the appropriate time.'*

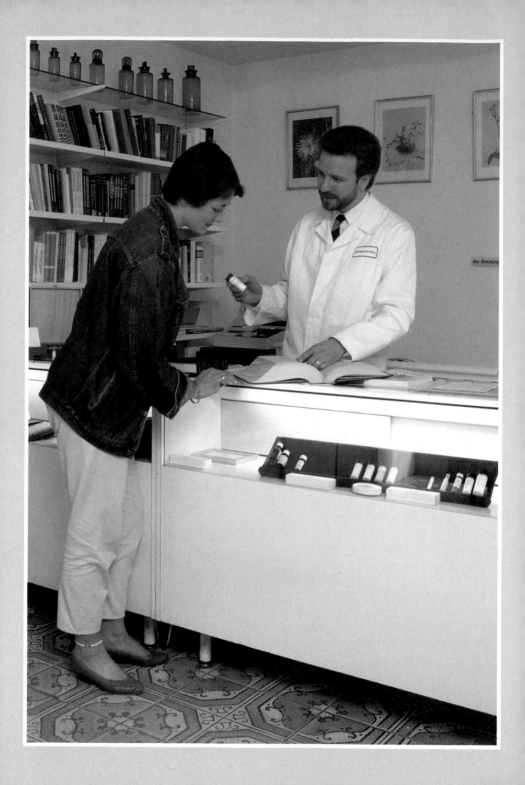

# 8

# FINDING
# AND CONSULTING
# A HOMEOPATH

That quotation comes from Dr Siegel's book *Love, Medicine and Miracles*. Dr Siegel, who is assistant Clinical Professor of Surgery at Yale Medical School, shows that when terminally-ill patients take control of their condition they can change, enrich, and often prolong their lives far beyond scientific expectation. In one chapter of the book, 'The Healing Partnership', he illustrates the importance of finding a physician who will encourage you in your healing process.

I can testify to this. I well remember the late Dr George Martos, under whose care I was born and spent my infancy and teenage years. 'Uncle George', who cared for all my family, was a hungarian, trained in Germany before World War II. He seldom used drugs or antibiotics, and tended to treat his patients with naturopathic techniques and diet. His smiling face was one I always looked forward to seeing when I was in bed, and his gentle voice and sense of humour were always cheering. He was a friend to his patients, someone they could tell their secrets to.

My mother told me that, when she was in labour with me, Dr Martos kept her company by walking up and down the hospital veranda (this was in India in midsummer) during the first stage. How many doctors have the time to do this nowadays?

### Making your choice

Dr Martos was an example of how valuable the right medical consultant can be, and you may be wondering how to choose the homeopathic practitioner who is right for you. Many people find their homeopathic practitioner through the recommendations of friends, a local health food shop, or a natural-health clinic. In this way you can select someone through his or her reputation – as a homeopath who gets results. This is indeed a very natural process, and one that works for many people. Your friends are likely to have similar interest and lifestyles to yourself, and for this reason the approach of the practitioner they go to is likely to suit you too. However, this may not always be the case.

If you do not find the attitude of your homeopathic practitioner supportive, or respectful of you as an individual, do not be afraid to say so. All health care practitioners have 'off days' like anyone else. They are not supermen or superwomen, however much they might like to be. So voice any dissatisfactions you may have, and ask the practitioner to

*Physicians must stop letting statistics determine their beliefs. Statistics are important when one is choosing the best therapy for a certain illness; but once that choice is made, they no longer apply to the individual. All patients must be accorded the conviction that they can get well, no matter what the odds.*

Bernie S. Siegel.

explain what is happening in your treatment.

If you are still not happy with the practitioner's attitude, .or handling of your treatment, ask yourself whether you have in fact hit on the practitioner who is right for you, or even whether some other therapy might suit you better. Remember that what you believe does affect your recovery, whatever therapy you are having. Your relationship with your practitioner may well affect your beliefs about your ability to get well again. Allow yourself to be guided by your own intuition and reactions when you consider who may be the best person to treat you.

## The problem of reticence

In Western countries we tend to be reticent about our private lives, and may overemphasize the confidentiality of a medical consultation, to the detriment of our own cures. We seldom see ourselves as others see us: I have often found the missing link in a case by talking to a spouse or a relative about the patient. In this way I have learned that the patient is actually behaving in a manner that is the opposite to what I have been led to believe during the consultation; or that signs and symptoms are far more or less severe than the patient describes. Relatives have told me of improvements in mood, energy, and other conditions that the patient is perhaps unaware of.

In Asian countries such as China and India, large populations live in crowded conditions, and people know each other's business. Consultations often take place with a crowd of other people – all waiting to see the practitioner – hovering around. Under such circumstances people are unable to be as secretive about their conditions as we are in the West. A cure may indeed be a group concern. Dr Monty Berman, an acupuncturist, ran an experimental co-operative practice in Lime Grove, London. At this clinic a patient's condition would be discussed initially in public in the reception area, enabling several people to say what they had observed about the patient before the kind of therapy was decided.

Such public consultation would not suit everybody, but do be willing to share your secrets with your practitioner even if there is a student sitting in the same room. Frankness is likely to speed your recovery, not only by making your case clearer to the practitioner, but also because sharing what you may consider to be a 'guilty' secret can be a very important step in letting go of any psychological blocks that may be impeding your recovery, or that may even be partly responsible for your condition.

Remember that homeopathic practitioners are used to hearing about a wide variety of unpleasant memories or embarrassing habits. They are not there to sit in judgement on you, but only to find the right remedy for you and help you to get well. And although it is part of a healer's job to encourage a healthy lifestyle, he or she should never try to moralize or to manipulate you. If you think that your practitioner is acting in this way towards you, you need to consider carefully whether you have made the right choice and whether you would be better advised to consult another practitioner who is more understanding.

You may also like to consider whether you want to see a male or female practitioner. Some people may disagree with this on the grounds of sexual discrimination. But to many patients it does make a difference. Some may feel very awkward telling a member of the opposite sex about certain matters, such as sexual difficulties, menstrual problems, or relationships with members of their family. Others find it easier to consult a member of the opposite sex about such things. The main thing is to decide which will work best for you.

*If you are hesitant about consulting a homeopath, it may help you to know that in practice visiting a homeopath is no different to visiting an orthodox family doctor. There will be no unfamiliar instruments. The only difference will be the number of questions the homeopath will ask before making a diagnosis.*

## Your own commitment

If you decide to try the homeopathic way to health, it is important that you are willing to make a commitment to the homeopathic process of cure. This involves time and understanding. If you have a chronic condition, for example, which has taken time to develop, it may take time to go – although the more willing you are to address the matter of your lifestyle and general health, the quicker this process should be. Remember the law of cure: do not rush for a course of antibiotics if an acute condition suddenly arises during treatment of a chronic illness. A homeopath can treat your acute condition as well, and will do so if necessary – although sometimes only simple nursing and adequate rest are required.

The advice of W. H. Murray (in another context) is worth quoting at this point:

> 'Until one is committed there is hesitancy, the chance to draw back, always ineffectiveness. Concerning all acts of initiative (and creation) there is one elementary truth, the ignorance of which kills countless ideas and splendid plans: that the moment one definitely commits oneself, the Providence moves too. All sorts of things occur to help one that would never otherwise have occurred.'

## Registers and regulations

Registers of both medical doctors who have become homeopaths, and homeopathic practitioners without a medical background, are available to the public in Britain, America and Europe. Addresses for British and American practitioners are given in Chapter 9. Indeed, wherever homeopathy is practised, there are societies whose aim is to promote information and regulate standards. Such registers are obviously useful if you do not know of a practitioner in your area. But although a register tells you something of the standard and training of a practitioner, it does not tell you what nature of person he or she is. Also, because the laws of the land vary so much in respect of the practitioners of therapies outside the orthodox medical establishment, there are many practitioners who have not yet registered themselves with a professional body, even though they may have been practising for a long time. Others choose not to have their names on a register, although they are members of a professional body.

In the UK, both medical doctors who have added homeopathic training to their orthodox qualifications, and practitioners who have trained for four years in homeopathy, are able to treat patients. Members of the Society of Homeopaths (address given in Chapter 9) must have attended a thorough four-year course, which covers philosophy, *Materia Medica,* therapeutics, case analysis and supervised practical work. In addition, professional homeopaths study anatomy, physiology, pathology and both conventional and alternative diagnostic methods. Common law allows you to go to whoever you choose for healing. Nevertheless, the law is also very clear that practitioners must not call themselves doctors unless they are medically qualified.

In some European countries homeopaths are able to practise legally, or under the 'umbrella' of a qualified physician. In other European countries homeopathy is illegal, but tolerated: there is so much demand for it that the authorities turn a blind eye to it, and there are few prosecutions. The laws and regulations are changing: the practice of homeopathy has recently been legalized in Norway, while in the Netherlands all mainstream therapies have been officially recognized, and patients can now claim for payment of fees under the Dutch health insurance scheme.

In the United States and Canada homeopaths may be medical doctors, licensed professionals such as chiropractors, nurses, midwives, dentists and naturopaths, or professional practitioners – all of whom will have undergone several years of training. There are still some legal restrictions – nurses, for example, may only prescribe homeopathic remedies under the supervision of a physician. And legal guidelines for professional homeopaths who have not undergone any other form of medical training are, at the time of writing, confused. But the tide is turning in favour of homeopathy. For example, due to public demand and some test cases fought in court, California's state legislature has changed the law. Citizens can now go directly to alternative health practitioners and do not have to be referred by a qualified physician.

Many doctors are becoming interested in homeopathy, and some people who initially trained as chiropractors are going on to become homeopaths as well. But strong opposition from the United States medical establishment means that there is still a long way to go in educating the general public to accept homeopathy.

### Homeopathy and the NHS in Britain

In Britain it is possible to obtain homeopathic treatment under the National Health Service. Unfortunately, in-depth homeopathic consultations cannot be given in the time that the average busy general practitioner allows for seeing a patient under the National Health Service. So many homeopathically trained doctors go on practising allopathy as usual, and use homeopathic remedies only in some situations, or if the patient specifically asks for homeopathic treatment.

Currently, both homeopathic and orthodox hospitals have long waiting lists. And since homeopathic hospitals entered the National Health Service in 1948, they are no longer purely homeopathic and provide orthodox treatment as well. If you decide to attend a homeopathic hospital, be prepared for a wait of up to six months for an appointment. You will not automatically get homeopathic treatment, so remember to ask for it. You may also find that you see a different practitioner each time, with several months between consultations.

It may be that in the future more alternative therapies, including the services of homeopathic practitioners, will be available under the National Health Service. However, it is difficult to practise good Hahnemannian homeopathy under the NHS as it is organized at present.

### Private homeopathic medicine

In Britain, America and a number of other countries, good homeopathic treatment is available privately from professional homeopathic practitioners (who have trained solely in this form of medicine) or qualified doctors who have given up practising allopathic medicine and are full-time homeopaths.

### What will going private cost?

In Britain the fee for an initial homeopathic consultation can be anything from £15 to £40, while in the United States the fee for an initial consultation is likely to be $100. The fee varies depending on the area in which the practitioner lives, the overheads of the practice, such as the wages of a receptionist and the rent of the premises. The number of years the homeopath has been in practice may also affect the scale of fees, although this is rarely a determining factor. Most homeopathic practitioners reduce their fees for the unemployed and senior citizens. After the first visit you will need several follow-up consultations costing from £7 to £20 a time, usually at monthly intervals until there is a good sign of improvement. After that you will need to attend only if you have a relapse, or some other disorder occurs. Telephone consultations for acute disorders such as influenza are generally charged at a reduced rate.

To some people these fees may seem enormous; to others, comparatively little. The charges are relative, and depend not only on your income, but also on how much your health is worth to you. However, some health insurance companies in Britain and America are now starting to include alternative and complementary medicine in their schemes. It is up to the public to demand that they all do so.

Many practitioners of alternative medicine and other complementary therapies have noticed that there is more commitment from the patients who pay than there is from those for whom they waive the fees. It is interesting to note that in a homeopathic clinic for the poor in Calcutta a token payment is made, even if it is only 1 pisa (equal to a fraction of a penny); this shows the commitment of the patient to the treatment, and appears to encourage better participation.

**Working together**

An increasing number of orthodox medical practitioners are referring patients to practitioners of other therapies, including homeopathy. A sympathetic doctor may well want to keep in touch with your homeopathic practitioner to follow the progress of your treatment, and to confer in cases where allopathic medication has already been prescribed for chronic ailments. The doctor can then advise on the gradual reduction of the allopathic medicine as the effect of the homeopathic treatment improves your health. Fortunately homeopathic medicines work through the 'blanket' of other drugs without causing difficulties from incompatibility, because they are working on a different level of energy; but treatment may take longer if both kinds of medicine are being taken simultaneously.

Even if your general practitioner is not sympathetic to homeopathic treatment, it is worth consulting him or her for some conditions when conventional Western diagnostic aids may be necessary. Homeopathic practitioners in Britain do not yet have the right to refer patients to hospitals for specialist diagnosis, such as X-rays and blood tests, although medically qualified homeopaths do. You should be willing to let your homeopathic practitioner have the name and address of your allopathic doctor (general practitioner); the practitioner may wish to write to your GP to say that you are having homeopathic treatment, and what it is.

Homeopathy needs people who have benefited by it to speak out, so that there will never again be the persecution of its practitioners that has continued since the days of Hahnemann. Tell other people – including your GP and specialist consultants – what homeopathy has done for you. Some patients refuse to tell their GPs that they have improved since starting homeopathic treatment for fear of upsetting them; this may be understandable, but it does not lend itself to the promotion of truth and clarity.

Remember: homeopathy works. If it is not working for you, try another practitioner who may see your case in a fresh light. Blame your practitioner if you must, or consider your own attitude. But don't blame homeopathy.

*Many homeopaths offer their patients a comprehensive service of health care, from consultation and diagnosis to making and dispensing the remedies.*

# 9

# USEFUL
# INFORMATION

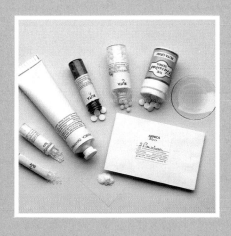

## USEFUL ADDRESSES

### Organizations

American Holistic Medical Association
2727 Fairview Avenue East, Seattle,
Washington 98102, MSA

American Institute of Homeopathy
1500 Massachusetts Avenue NW, Washington
DC 20005, USA

Association for Holistic Health
PO Box 12407, La Jolla, California 92037, USA

British Homeopathic Association
27a Devonshire Street, London W1N 1RJ, UK

Council for Complementary & Alternative
Medicine (CCAM)
Suite 1, 19a Cavendish Square, London W1M
9AD, UK

Foundation for Homeopathic Education and
Research
5916 Chabot Crest, Oakland, California 94618,
USA

Glasgow Homeopathic Hospital
1000 Great Western Road, Glasgow G12, UK

Hahnemann Medical Clinic
1918 Bonita Street, Berkeley, California 94704,
USA

The Hahnemann Society
Humane Education Centre, Avenue Lodge,
Bounds Green Road, London N22 4EU, UK

Homeopathic Development Foundation Ltd
Harcourt House, 19a Cavendish Square, London
W1M 9AD, UK

Institute for Complementary Medicine (ICM)
21 Portland Place, London W1N 3AF, UK

International Foundation for Homeopathy
2366 Eastlake Avenue East #301, Seattle,
Washington 98102, USA

John Bastyr College of Naturopathic Medicine

1408 NE 45th Street, Seattle, Washington 98105,
USA

National College of Naturopathic Medicine
11231 SE Market Street, Portland, Oregon 97216,
USA

National Foundation for Holistic Medicine
66 Milton Road, Rye, New York,
NY 10580, USA

Research Council for Complementary Medicine
Suite 1, 19a Cavendish Square, London
W1M 9AD, UK

The Royal London Homeopathic Hospital
Great Ormond Street, London WC1N 3HR, UK

The Society of Homeopaths
2 Artizan Road, Northampton, NN1 4HU, UK

### Homeopathic suppliers

Ainsworths' Homeopathic Pharmacy
38 New Cavendish Street, London W1M 7LH,
UK

Boericke and Tafel Inc.
1011 Arch Street, Philadelphia, PA 19107, USA

Freeman's Pharmaceutical & Homeopathic
Chemists
7 Eaglesham Road, Clarkston, Glasgow, UK

The Galen Pharmacy (J.A. Eiles, MPS),
Homeopathic & Dispensing Chemists, 1 South
Terrace, South Street, Dorchester, Dorset, UK

Homeopathic Educational Services
2124 Kittredge Street, Berkeley, California
94704, USA

The Homeopathic Pharmacopeia Convention of
the United States
1500 Massachusetts Avenue NW, Washington
DC 20005, USA

A. Nelson & Co Ltd
73 Duke Street, London W1M 6BY, UK

## ACKNOWLEDGMENTS

The publishers would like to thank the following organizations and individuals for their kind permission to reproduce the illustrations in this book:

**Ace/Michael Bluestone:** 145, 148 **Ainsworths' Homeopathic Pharmacy:** 44, 48, 49, 50 **Allsport:** 42 **Ancient Art & Architecture Collection:** 111, 125 **Bubbles Photo Library/Loisjoy Thurstun:** 98, 103 **Camera Press/Michael Blackman:** 137 **J Allan Cash:** 99, 112 **Bruce Coleman Ltd/Hans Reinhard:** 127 **Mary Evans Picture Library:** 35, 39, 117, 123, 132, 122 **Robert Harding Picture Library/Carol Jopp:** 67 **Impact/Sally Fear:** 25 **London Features International:** 13 left **Octopus Publishing Group:** Steve Lyne 26,/Laurie Evans 27 **The Photographers Library:** 72 **Popperfoto:** 34, 141 **Ann Ronan Picture Library:** 30, 37, 41, 46 above, 128, 134 **Science Photo Library:** John Durham 11, 20,/31, 36, 40,/Thelma Moss 109,/David Parker 113,/Andrew McClenaghan 120,/Paul Biddle & Tim Malyon 121 **Tony Stone Associates:** 14, 115, 106 **Jennie Woodcock:** 23 below **Zefa:** 17, 19, 21, 28, 33, 82, 87, 88, 89

**The following photographs were specially taken by Peter Chadwick:** 6, 7 (Courtesy Hahnemann Museum) 2, 10, 23 above, 45, 46 below, 52, 57, 70, 74, 75, 77, 78, 90, 101, 108, 118, 144, 153, 154

Our thanks to the **Westminster Natural Health Centre, London** and also to Nelson Pharmacies Ltd and Ainsworths' Homeopathic Pharmacy for their help with these photographs.

**Illustrations** by Elaine Anderson

**Editor** Viv Croot   **Art Editor** Alyson Kyles
**Coordinating Editor** Camilla Simmons   **Designer** Malcolm Smythe

**Production** Alyssum Ross   **Picture research** Christina Weir